Roger Williams
The Church and the State

OTHER BOOKS BY EDMUND S. MORGAN

The Genuine Article: A Historian Looks at Early America

Benjamin Franklin

Inventing the People: The Rise of Popular Sovereignty in England and America

The Puritan Family: Religion and Domestic Relations in Seventeenth-Century New England

Virginians at Home: Family Life in the Eighteenth Century

The Stamp Act Crisis: Prologue to Revolution (with Helen M. Morgan)

The Birth of the Republic

The Puritan Dilemma: The Story of John Winthrop

The Genius of George Washington

The Meaning of Independence: John Adams, George Washington, and Thomas Jefferson

The Challenge of the American Revolution

American Slavery, American Freedom: The Ordeal of Colonial Virginia

The Gentle Puritan: A Life of Ezra Stiles

Visible Saints: The History of a Puritan Idea

So What About History

EDITED WORKS

Not Your Usual Founding Father: Selected Readings from Benjamin Franklin

Prologue to Revolution: Sources and Documents on the Stamp Act Crisis

The Diary of Michael Wigglesworth: The Conscience of a Puritan

Puritan Political Ideas

The Founding of Massachusetts: Historians and the Sources

The American Revolution: Two Centuries of Interpretation

Roger Williams
The Church and the State

Edmund S. Morgan

W · W · Norton & Company · New York · London

Manufacturing by RR Donnelley, Bloomsburg
Production manager: Devon Zahn

Library of Congress Catalog Card Number: 67-25999

ISBN 978-0-393-30403-9 pbk.

W. W. Norton & Company, Inc., 500 Fifth Avenue, New York, N.Y. 10110
www.wwnorton.com

W. W. Norton & Company Ltd., Castle House, 75/76 Wells Street, London
W1T 3QT

1 2 3 4 5 6 7 8 9 0

Contents

Preface to the New Edition

Did the founding fathers of the United States believe in separation of church and state? Of course. Did they not secure an amendment to their Constitution, stating that "Congress shall make no law respecting an establishment of religion, or prohibiting the free exercise thereof"? Thomas Jefferson declared in 1802 that these words placed "a wall of eternal separation between church and state." It is nevertheless fair to ask how high Jefferson and the other founding fathers believed that wall to rise. Not so high as to prevent the early United States House of Representatives from offering its chambers to various denominations of Christians for Sunday services. It did not prevent most of the separate states, in their first constitutions, from restricting political rights (voting and holding office) to Christians or even Protestant Christians. In New England until 1833 state governments levied taxes to pay ministers' salaries, by which the populace as a whole were required to support Christianity whether they liked it or not. The United States Army, like the other branches of the military, commissions and pays chaplains of various denominations, without serious questions raised about this particular form of sponsoring religion.

The wall is obviously not impenetrable and never has been. Although in the twentieth century the Supreme Court began closing some of the chinks in that wall, its effectiveness has always depended more on pragmatic exigencies than on the philosophical principles that Jefferson and James Madison sought to place at its foundation. Most of the English colonies in America were founded in the seventeenth century with a single religion as the official faith. But dissent and dissension among the descendants of the first settlers, together with immigration from European countries, produced such a variety of beliefs and churchly institutions that by 1776 no single denomination could command the allegiance of a majority of the citizens of the United States or any of its constituent states. Since no one church could aspire to be the established religion of the Americans, the founders conjured up a wall of separation, however porous, to maintain the peace. As early as 1767 a devout New England clergyman, himself a Congregationalist, could celebrate the existence of an array of churches as a positive virtue: "Our grand security," Ezra Stiles wrote, "is in the multitude of sects and the public Liberty necessary for them to cohabit together. . . . This and this only will learn us wisdom *not to persecute one another.*"

In this situation the degree of separation between church and state prescribed by the First Amendment was not much more than already existed. There was no real opposition to the amendment, which became law in 1792. But long before the proliferation of sects and denominations, special courage and a special kind of zeal were needed to demand that a government give up the power it derived directly and indirectly from sponsoring the church. In the seventeenth century Roger Williams, a Puritan minister, had both the zeal and the courage, and he had something else, a fertile mind that drove him to examine accepted ideas and carry them to unacceptable conclusions. One conclusion he reached very early was that the welfare of both church and state required an impenetrable barrier between them.

Separation between church and state was seemingly an accepted idea in early New England. The first settlers had gone there to escape the severe penalties that the state imposed on their dissent from a church whose clergy they found too worldly and too inclined to water down religious doctrines. As will be seen in the pages below, they took pains to keep their own governments free from clerical control. But they did not attempt the total separation that Williams came to think was essential to the very being of both institutions.

Williams was not a rebel by nature. Wherever he went people liked him, including the founders of Massachusetts Bay, who welcomed him with open arms when he arrived in 1631. But he was probably the most original thinker to join them and a powerful thinker who could not keep his ideas to himself. It was probably inevitable that men in positions of authority in the Bay Colony would eventually find his ideas concerning the state's authority to prescribe religion too dangerous to allow him to remain among them. Five years after he came to Massachusetts they expelled him. He went to Rhode Island, still a wilderness, and established there a haven for other original thinkers, with a government committed to keeping its hands off any churches that people there might gather.

This book is not about Roger Williams as the founder of Rhode Island. It is an attempt to reconstruct his journey from acceptable to unacceptable ideas, from the ideas he shared with other New England ministers to new intellectual territory where they would not or dared not follow him. It is not simply about the wall he would have built between church and state, but about the development of his understanding of what the church is or should be and what the state is or should be. His thinking on these subjects, too disturbing for seventeenth-century Massachusetts, still has the power to disturb twenty-first-century America. It poses a challenge to all those who would allow a church to meddle in politics and equally to those who would allow the state to meddle with the teachings of a church.

Edmund S. Morgan
July 2006
New Haven, Connecticut

Author's Note

This is a book I had not intended to write. When the complete publications of Roger Williams were reissued a few years ago, I took the opportunity to read them consecutively and systematically. As I read and reread, I gradually recognized that I had formerly misunderstood and misjudged the man, and I thought that many other historians had done so too. His single-minded zeal in support of every cause he espoused has drawn attention away from the structure of his thought. Although Williams usually wrote polemically, in the heat of the contests of his day, his ideas exhibit an intricate and beautiful symmetry, broken only on the rare occasions when he succumbed to the temptation to argue from a position that he had himself rejected but knew that his opponents accepted. I have tried to reconstruct the course of his thought and to expose the symmetry of the ideas that lay behind the polemics. My wife, as always, has helped me more than I can say. If we have succeeded, the book belongs to Roger Williams.

E. S. M.

Roger Williams
The Church and the State

I

Englishman, Puritan, Separatist

Roger Williams lived in what he called "wonderful, searching, disputing and dissenting times." [1] Three centuries later the description still seems accurate. From the accession of James Stuart in 1603 to the Glorious Revolution of 1688 Englishmen thought long and hard about authority, both in church and in state, and they tried their thoughts in action. None thought longer or harder, none searched, disputed, or dissented more earnestly than Williams himself, and none was more ready to try his thoughts in action.

The facts of his life, so far as they are known, have been often and ably related: his education at Charterhouse and Cambridge, his exodus to Massachusetts in the first winter of the Puritan settlement there, his expulsion from the colony for his novel ideas, his founding of Rhode Island as a refuge for religious dissent, and his subsequent career as leader and defender of the colony and spokesman for freedom of conscience in both England and America. The history is an honorable one and has earned a place in the classic accounts of the American past. It will not be repeated here, for this is neither a biography of Williams nor a study of his colony, but an attempt to trace the way he thought.[2]

Williams did what he did because of what he thought. Never was a man of action more an intellectual. But in the progression of his ideas we can find much more than an explanation of what he did. We can find a man thinking in an age of great intellectual expansion—not an ordinary man, for ordinary men seldom think, not a typical man, for in the end hardly anyone agreed with him, but a man nevertheless who was driven by the same intellectual forces that moved other men of that restless time. Williams was a Puritan, and in him we can watch Puritan thought exploding, hurling itself outward to its ultimate limits. The diverse internal energies that other Puritans were able to restrain and bring into uneasy harmony went unchecked in Williams. If we follow him as he allowed the force of his ideas to sweep him from the conventional to the original, from orthodoxy to heresy, we will enjoy the spectacle of a great religious imagination at work, and at the same time we will see exposed some of the hidden conflicts that tormented every Puritan.

The spectacle is not easily observed. Roger Williams' writings are voluminous, filling seven volumes in the latest edition,[3] but they are couched in a syntax that often defies analysis: Williams could stretch a sentence to several paragraphs before bringing himself to a predicate. What is worse, for anyone interested in the way he got from one idea to another, his surviving writings, other than a few letters, were all written after his thought had reached maturity. The earliest was published in 1643, seven years after his banishment from Massachusetts. Nearly everything we know about what Williams thought before he left Massachusetts must be inferred from these later writings and from the brief and biased reports written by his opponents at the time.[4]

A reconstruction of his intellectual development must therefore be conjectural. The conjecture may nevertheless carry a high degree of probability. Williams was a man of his time and very much a part of it. His letters reveal a warm man, outgoing and friendly, by temperament more prone to agreement than to the disagreements that his intellectual questing drove him to. The direction of his thought may thus be traced in relation to the ideas from which he started, the ideas he learned from those around him, from the masters at whose feet he sat, from the men with whom he worked and talked before he talked himself into intellectual solitude. His thinking progressed not by opposing accepted ideas, but by pursuing them through their implications to conclusions that his contemporaries could not or would not accept. The ideas with which he began are therefore visible everywhere in his mature writings, and clear signs of his most novel conclusions are already discernible in statements attributed to him during his early years in Massachusetts. From these alleged statements and from his own writings we can chart the logical, and in some measure the chronological, course of his thinking, especially his thinking about the two subjects that drew his primary attention, the church and the state. Roger Williams did write about other matters, but his treatment of them was conventional and static. The history of his ideas attempted in the succeeding pages will deal only with the way he thought about the church, the state, and the relationship between them.

The Importance of Being English

Roger Williams was born in London, probably in 1603. Almost nothing is known of his childhood beyond the fact that his father was a "merchant tailor" and that his mother came of a family of gentry in St. Albans. From a letter that Williams wrote in 1652 we know that he was befriended by the great jurist, Sir Edward Coke, who as a governor of the Charterhouse School may have secured Williams' admission in 1621. The records of Pembroke Hall, Cambridge show that he entered there two years later, received his B.A. in 1627, and remained to study theology. From two more letters we know that in 1629 he became chaplain in the family of Sir William Masham at High Laver, Essex. In December of that year the parish register records his marriage to Mary Barnard, a maid in a neighboring household. Within a little more than a year they were both in New England.[5]

Although so little is known of Williams' early life, the fact that it was lived in England at the opening of the seventeenth century tells us much, for Englishmen in the reign of Elizabeth had acquired a special set of ideas about England and England's place in the history of the world. Williams was to reject those ideas, but to understand what he put in their place we must begin with what he rejected.

Englishmen have always had special ideas about England, but the men who had lived under Elizabeth had reason for thinking that theirs was both an extraordinary country and an extraordinary time. The great queen aroused in them an enthusiasm that made England more than a land and her reign more than a moment of triumph. Her subjects breathed an atmosphere of expectation, and they turned to history in order to locate themselves. They wanted to discover the significance, in some grand scheme of things, of the great events taking place around them and of the greater ones that they thought must be coming.

For these men, the fundamental source book of history, as of all truth, was the Bible. In it could be read not only the past but the present and future as well, and no part of it held more clues to the destiny of England in the sixteenth and seventeenth centuries than the Book of Revelation. Theologians and scholars gave their days and nights to Revelation, in order to translate its cryptic messages into a history of Europe and England. When did the tyranny of Antichrist begin, or had it? When would it end, or had it? And when was or would be the fall of Babylon and the thousand-year reign of the saints with Christ? The outline of England's history as seen by English Protestants had begun to take shape in the answers to such questions even before Elizabeth ascended the throne. On one thing they nearly all agreed: the pope was Antichrist and the Roman Church was the Great Whore of Babylon. The crucial question was how long the power of Rome would last. As the glory of Elizabeth's reign mounted and her seamen defied the cohorts of Antichrist all over the world, Englishmen persuaded themselves that they were a favored people, a people whom God had cast in a role paralleled only by that of the Jews before the coming of Christ. They believed they were the successors of Israel, an elect nation destined to lead the world back to God's true religion and end the tyranny of Antichrist.[6]

The story began with the planting of the gospel in England, not by missionaries from Rome, as had once been supposed, but by emissaries from the apostles themselves. From that time forward, the history of England had been a history of good kings who protected the true faith and of misguided kings whose evil counsellors led them to betray England's mission. In this interpretation, which found classic expression in the many editions of Foxe's *Book of Martyrs,* the successive invasions of the island became attacks by heathen intruders on native Christians. Through the efforts of good kings and other heroes, the true faith was somehow preserved, the more easily from the fourth century to the fourteenth because this was the thousand-year period, foretold in Revelation, when Satan was chained up.

With the opening of the fourteenth century, Satan was let loose and Antichrist began his tyranny over the Church. The history of true Christians ever since had been written in the blood of martyrs. Nowhere had their blood flowed more freely than in England, for it was here that the truth had been most carefully preserved and from here that it spread back to the Continent after having been nearly extinguished there. The first prophet of the Reformation, according to English Protestants, was not Martin Luther but John Wyclif: Wyclif begot Huss and Huss begot Luther. England, then, was the stronghold and fountainhead of true faith. The people had suffered heavily under Mary, whose evil counsellors betrayed them to Rome. During the period of Mary's rule some Protestant leaders had called upon Englishmen to overthrow her, lest in addition to persecution they be made to suffer the wrath of God for complicity in their queen's betrayal of the nation's divine mission. But God saw fit to remove Mary without assistance and then sent Elizabeth to protect and lead His chosen people in the battle against Antichrist. When evil bishops urged the new queen to subject herself to the pope, she had replied in the words of Joshua, "I and my house will serve the lord"; she and her people were in covenant not with Rome but with God.[7]

In the past, God's help had enabled England's pious monarchs to lead His people successfully through countless troubles. What might He have in store for them now? Since He had removed an Antichristian monarch and installed the great Elizabeth, perhaps the culmination of history was at hand. When God raised a mighty storm to help Elizabeth's fleet throw back the armada of Antichristian invaders from Spain in 1588, some Englishmen could even read in the event a premonition of the millennium, when England would lead all nations to the Kingdom of God.

As long as Elizabeth lived, Englishmen persisted in their optimism, but it became increasingly difficult after 1588 to detect the rising tide of godliness that should signify a people recovering from the attacks of Antichrist and about to lead the nations in introducing the Kingdom of God on earth. Although the most eager English reformers, the Puritans, combined their tributes to the queen with detailed instructions about the proper way to play her destined role, Elizabeth ignored them and took no steps to eradicate the visible remains of Roman corruption that the Puritans pointed out to her in the Church of England. By the time her successor took the throne and began to talk about harrying the Puritans out of the land, it was apparent to many Englishmen that there had been a mistake in their reading of history and that God's chosen people had more buffeting to suffer from Antichrist.

The question of England's place in history had thus been reopened at the time when Roger Williams was growing up. Even in the face of James I's apparent hostility to righteousness, it was still possible to cling to the old view of England's destiny but adjust the time scale to place the ultimate triumph of the elect nation at a greater distance in the future: James I could be regarded as merely another misguided king who failed in his duty to keep the people of God on the true path. The majority of English Protestants doubtless made this adjustment. They chided king and country for backsliding and pleaded for reformation. But some took the harder alternative and worked out new meanings for Revelation and a new philosophy of history. It is impossible to say how early Roger Williams turned his attention to history, but there can be no doubt that when he did, he took the second alternative and arrived at some answers of his own about England's role in the divine scheme of things.

Williams never specifically stated in any surviving writing at what point he thought Satan had been chained up or unleashed. But Williams, in direct contrast to most of his contemporaries, did believe that in the fourth century the Christian church had begun a long "sleep" in which Satan had been active and successful.[8] With his assistance Antichrist had triumphed, in England as much as anywhere else. Williams had the confidence of every Protestant that Christ would come again, subdue Satan, and destroy Antichrist, but he was not sanguine about the imminence of the date, nor did he find reason to suppose that the millennial headquarters would be located in England. Williams had an unusual capacity for looking squarely at facts, and neither the facts of English history nor the evidence of Scripture seemed to him to support the popular view of England's appointed role in the struggle with Antichrist. His reasoning on this subject and the other intellectual discoveries that accompanied it will be discussed in a later chapter. That his conclusions deprived him of the comfort of thinking his own country uniquely favored was characteristic of the man. Williams' ideas seldom brought him comfort.

Puritanism

Williams was born an Englishman; he became a Puritan. When does not matter. It was probably at Cambridge University, but possibly long before. To have been a Puritan in the first three decades of the seventeenth century may not have been very different from simply being an Englishman. A recent exhaustive study of English Protestantism from 1570 to 1640 led the authors to conclude in effect that there was no such thing as a Puritan, that the ideas and attitudes generally attributed to Puritans were shared in varying degrees by all English Protestants.[9] But the most hotly contested religious differences among Christians have often been differences of degree; the shift from orthodoxy to heresy may be no more than a shift of emphasis. And however alike English Protestants of the early seventeenth century may appear from the perspective of the present, at the time they looked different to each other; and a part of them—a rather large part—earned from the others the epithet "Puritan."

At the root of the difference between Puritans and other Englishmen was a deeper sense among Puritans of the great obstacle that lay between man and salvation. The Puritans insisted that man must keep the obstacle in full view and recognize that no saint or angel, no church or priest or bishop could carry him over it. Nor could his own efforts, with or without their assistance. The obstacle was man's depravity, unavoidably inherited from his first ancestor. The Puritan Roger Williams learned that he had been born hopelessly, desperately evil and that only God's merciful saving grace, dispensed through Christ without relation to merit, could save him from the eternal damnation that all men deserved. He also learned that God would save fewer men than He damned.

Other Englishmen recognized the existence of human depravity but allowed somewhat more efficacy to the church and to a man's own efforts in overcoming his depravity. The Puritan view would perhaps have been debilitating if it had left men not only helpless but also without a hint of God's intentions toward them. But Puritan theologians had taught men how to hope and strive for God's mercy. The theologians had examined the process of salvation and broken it down into a series of events occurring in successive stages within the human soul. By searching his own soul daily, a man might determine whether or not the crucial process was under way within him. The determination could never be made with absolute certainty (a man could easily err in his diagnosis), nor could the process of salvation be completed before death. As long as a man breathed, depravity would drag him down; but if his internal history followed the accepted pattern, he had reason to hope that he was among the elect who would stand at the right hand of Christ on the last day.[10]

Different theologians identified a greater or lesser number of distinct stages in an individual's redemption, but the general pattern was always the same. It always included near the beginning a response to the preaching of the Word. If God meant to save a man, He always exposed him to His Word. By the Word a man could comprehend the full perfection of righteousness that God demanded and measure the failure of his own achievement. The result that followed (if a man understood and "improved" the lesson of the Word) was an overwhelming sense of remorse and regret, which might be divided into several stages, including conviction (a recognition of guilt), humiliation, contrition, and repentance. All these a man might experience and yet go no further, for these might come by a man's own efforts. If, however, he was one of God's elect, at some point in his grief the Holy Spirit would enter his soul, bringing saving grace. Its entrance was followed by further transformations in the soul, by faith, justification, adoption, sanctification (a striving for righteous actions in daily life), and assurance.

Roger Williams probably learned the details of this pattern of salvation at Cambridge, for some of the great Puritan theologians who elaborated it had taught there.[11] That he learned it somewhere is certain, for he himself prepared a little manual for his wife, to help her recognize the movements of the Spirit within her. It was like a hundred other manuals of the kind. Although no two theologians divided the various stages in quite the same way, Williams' morphology of conversion, as outlined in his *Experiments of Spiritual Life and Health*,[12] varied in no important detail from that of other Puritans. And the progress of his thought about church and state never shook the orthodoxy of his ideas about salvation.

As a Puritan, Williams also learned another vocabulary to describe God's dealings with men. When Englishmen read the Bible, they found that God had sometimes bound himself in agreements or "covenants," and as Puritan and other Protestant theologians explored the mysteries of divinity, they found it convenient to explain the actions of omnipotence in terms of such covenants.[13] God had made a "covenant of works" with Adam, offering Adam salvation in return for perfect obedience. But Adam broke the covenant and left his posterity unable to obey and deprived of eternal life. God then made another covenant, the "covenant of grace," with Abraham and his seed, promising salvation in return for faith. Abraham's seed was the people of Israel, and so God had a covenant with Israel. He also made a "covenant of redemption" with Christ, and after

Christ fulfilled that covenant, God offered the covenant of grace to all who attained faith.

Covenant theology, as this manner of speaking has come to be called, was popular with Puritans, perhaps because it brought the infinite within the realm of comprehension, or seemed to. It also seemed to mitigate the helplessness of man, but this was not the intention. The covenant of grace, by which alone a man could be saved, was not really within the grasp of human effort. The faith which it demanded was the product of that process of conversion already described, in which man could act only by the aid of the Holy Spirit. The covenant of grace was a figure of speech, a way of describing the relationship to God of a man whom God had chosen to save. It was a covenant in which God fulfilled both parts of the agreement. Roger Williams, who was never one to minimize the powers of divinity or the impotence and depravity of man, had no trouble accepting covenant theology.[14] In this, as in most matters of theology, he remained at one with the Puritanism that was taught alike at Cambridge, England and Cambridge, Massachusetts.

Covenant theology bore no necessary relationship to ideas about church or state, but possible connections were obvious. For men accustomed to a God who made covenants, a God who had in fact bound himself in covenant with the whole people of Israel, it was not difficult to think of England as the successor of Israel, another whole people in covenant with God. The idea blended easily with one that had become a commonplace among political thinkers, namely that the state was the product of a covenant among men, between a king and his people or among the people themselves. This political covenant or social contract, though often thought to be re-enacted in the king's coronation oath, was largely imaginary, a convenient fiction, and it required no great additional stretch of the imagination to see God as being in some way a party to it. Since even the covenant of grace was a figure of speech, a national covenant with God could be a way of stating that England, like Israel, had a national obligation to obey God's laws. Such a covenant being only implicit, its terms could not of course be precisely known (surely it did not provide that every Englishman would be saved); but the analogy of Israel and England was pleasing to Englishmen, and most of them, whether of Puritan or Anglican cast, were content to leave it comfortably vague.

A number of English Puritans (those who later came to be known as Congregationalists or Independents) assimilated covenant theology far more specifically into their thinking about the church than about the state.[15] In the eyes of these Puritans—and Williams was initially among them—a church was the product of a covenant. Like the covenant in which the state presumably originated, a church covenant was a covenant among men, to which God was thought to be somehow a party. In some cases the founders stated explicitly that they were covenanting both with one another and with God. Those who believed that a church originated in a covenant also believed that a church was a company of visible saints, that is of the putative elect, who gathered to nourish the faith that the Spirit had started in them. Christ himself had prescribed the manner of their worship and instituted the sacrament of the Lord's Supper as a symbol of His presence. Only those to whom God had extended the covenant of grace could profit by this holy rite, and properly only they could join in the covenant of His church. It was not difficult, therefore, to think of a church covenant as an extension or external expression of the covenant of grace.

The implications of this conception of the church were

many and not fully recognized by those who first described it. For English Puritans who accepted it, and especially for ministers, the initial difficulty was to reconcile it with the actual Church of England to which they belonged. That church was almost as inclusive a body as the English state. It was not composed of visible saints but of saints and sinners alike. And if it was founded on a covenant, that covenant was only implicit, like the one on which the state supposedly rested. To overcome this difficulty a Puritan minister might gather a select group from his congregation and form a kind of church within a church. The group would make an explicit covenant together and might take the Lord's Supper in private meetings apart from the rest of the church. Puritan ministers were generally content to preach and pray with all the parish, but they tried to restrict the Lord's Supper, so far as possible, to men who could be counted as within the covenant of grace. They emphasized in books and sermons that the sacrament should be taken only by persons who could detect the stirrings of saving grace within them, and many of the manuals they wrote to assist the hopeful in this matter had as an immediate object to help men determine whether or not they were worthy of the Lord's Supper. The ministers might thus by persuasion reserve that rite for the saints. Ministers and groups who followed such procedures were in effect congregationalists within an episcopal church. Many of them expressly argued that there was no church larger than the number of visible saints that could gather in one meeting for worship, that all but saints should be excluded from the church, that there could be no minister except one chosen by the members of a particular church, that there should be, in other words, no church hierarchy, no church courts, no bishops, deans, or archbishops.[16]

To hold such beliefs and remain minister to an English

parish was awkward. While the minister of a parish church could urge the unconverted to refrain from the Lord's Supper, he could not properly deny it to men who lived decent lives but refused to worry about their souls. And the offering of the sacrament to a private meeting of saints was certainly of questionable legality. The select group who joined in covenant could not really be a church, nor could the minister be truly their pastor, for he, and they too, must submit to the orders of his superiors in the church hierarchy. And among the orders issuing from these pretenders were a host of instructions for ceremonies and rituals that Puritans could not find authorized in the Word of God.

In the face of these difficulties and contradictions one solution was obvious: leave the Church of England altogether and form new, separate churches. Beginning as early as the 1570's a number of Puritans did just that and earned the name of Separatists. Sometime after his graduation from Cambridge and before his arrival in Massachusetts, Roger Williams became a Separatist.

The route by which Williams arrived at Separatism was evidently that which another minister, John Canne, described a few years later.[17] Canne argued that the nonseparating Puritans held the same opinions as Separatists about the nature of the church. The difference between them was that Separatists practiced what they preached. By adhering scrupulously to his own principles, Canne said, a Puritan must sooner or later arrive at a recognition that neither the so-called Church of England nor any of its parish assemblies was a true church of Christ. Anyone reaching this position must separate. Williams agreed, and there is an evident autobiographical note in his later comment: "I beleeve that there hardly hath ever been a conscientious Seperatist, who was not first a Puritan: for (as Mr. Can hath unanswerably proved) the grounds and principles of the Puritans against Bishops and Ceremonies, and prophanes of people professing Christ, and the necessitie of Christs flock and discipline, must necessarily, if truely followed, lead on to, and inforce a separation from such wayes, worships, and Worshippers, to seek out the true way of Gods worship according to Christ Jesus." [18] Williams was to spend his life seeking out the true way of God's worship according to Christ Jesus. Separatism provided his point of departure, a last meeting place where he could join with others engaged on the same mission.

Separatism

No Christian could desert a church of Christ. On that Catholic and Protestant, Puritan and Separatist were agreed. A man who called himself a Christian and deserted the church was no Christian. But a Christian could and must desert a society that falsely claimed the name of church. The first distinguishing mark of a Separatist was his contention that the Church of England which he had deserted was no church of Christ.

Separatists reached this conclusion by several avenues of reasoning.[19] It was acknowledged by all Protestants that the Church of Rome was the church of Antichrist; and under Mary Tudor, from 1553 to 1558, the Church of England had been the Church of Rome. Whether it had ever been a true church, under Edward or Henry or in the first centuries of the Christian era, was to the Separatist a moot question. It was enough that under Mary the so-called church had belonged to Antichrist. On the accession of Elizabeth, as if by the blast of a trumpet, this Antichristian body had been proclaimed a church of Christ.

A church, the Separatists believed, could not be made so casually. In England many of the old "mass-priests" had assumed the name of ministers of Christ with scarcely an interruption in their chanting. Neither clergy nor laity had made so much as a show of repentance for their years of service against Christ in his enemy's synagogue. Such a people were no church but still the tools of Antichrist.

The Church of England was a national church, another contradiction in terms. Though Israel had been a national church, the Separatists insisted that a church of Christ could be no larger than a congregation, for this was the only kind of church that Christ and his apostles had recognized. Although not all Puritans agreed with the Separatists about the limits of a church's size, a great many did, and all agreed that the national hierarchy of bishops and archbishops was superfluous. Not merely superfluous, said the Separatists, but Antichristian. And this hierarchy exercised control over the parishes, the only units claiming the name of church that could possibly have deserved it by Separatist standards of size. They did not, however, deserve it: they were not churches but simply "assemblies," because of their subjection to the hierarchy and because they did not rest on voluntary covenants among visible saints.

The greatest defect of the Church of England, sufficient in the eyes of Separatists to destroy its claims, was its promiscuous membership. A church must be formed out of visible saints, and it must sustain their sanctity by the exercise of discipline, admonishing members who fell into wickedness and excommunicating those who proved incorrigible. Other Puritans agreed that a church ought to exclude the wicked and discipline its members when they lapsed into wickedness, but the Separatists made this exercise of discipline an essential mark of the church. Without it no church could exist. In England discipline was in the hands not of individual churches but of ecclesiastical courts, which used it more as a source of income than as a means of maintaining purity of membership. As the Separatist minister John Robinson put it, they played with excommunication like a child with a rattle, invoking it against good men for trivial offenses (in order to collect a large fee for restoration to good standing) and letting adulterers go scot free.[20] An organization that treated discipline in this way could not be a church of Christ.

In forming churches of their own, the Separatists strove to avoid the mistakes that they thought had annulled the church of Christ in England. They engaged with one another in explicit church covenants, repenting their former sins and agreeing to conduct themselves in work and worship by the laws of God. To guarantee that their churches would be built of "living stones," they required every member not only to subscribe the covenant and to lead a visibly godly life under the discipline of the church but also to make a profession or confession of faith, stating his belief in essential Christian doctrines. One of the early Separatist church covenants contained an express denunciation of the Antichristian so-called Church of England.[21] In general, however, the fact that a man was willing to leave that church probably made an express rejection of it seem superfluous. Indeed, willingness to join a Separatist church and suffer the hardships that went with membership in an illegal organization must also have been accepted as prima-facie evidence of a man's spiritual worthiness to join, for so far as can now be told, candidates for membership in the Separatist churches of England and Holland (where many fled to escape the consequences of defying the king and his bishops) were not required by any specific test to prove that they were regenerate.

The aim of the Separatists was nevertheless to make the

visible church an approximation of the eternal, invisible church. Like many Christians before and since, they were impressed with Paul's injunction, "come out from among them, and be ye separate." [22] They wanted to be separate not merely from the Church of England but from the world, which in the existing epoch was subjugated to Antichrist. They recognized that as individuals they must live in civil society and engage in the normal activities by which men made a living, but as members of Christ's church they were wary of becoming too closely involved in the ways of the world. Ordinarily they were people of humble circumstance and looked upon worldly success with some suspicion. In particular they were suspicious of wealthy clergymen and costly church buildings. Although their own ministers could not have gained salaries from the state anyhow, they made it a matter of principle that ministers subsist on their own labors or on voluntary contributions.

They were suspicious, too, of clergymen with authority. Authority in the hands of Anglican clergymen had been an effective way to acquire wealth and an ineffective way to maintain church discipline. The Separatists, in their own churches, minimized the role of the ministry and elevated that of the membership. The members administered church discipline. They also appointed the minister and could dismiss him. In the Separatist view, a minister became a minister only through election by a particular congregation. A church could exist without him but not he without a church. If he left the congregation or they dismissed him, he ceased altogether to be a minister. Although the Separatists thought a minister desirable for every church and agreed with other Puritans that he ought to be a man of learning, they emphasized the value of "prophesying," that is, of preaching by lay members of the church; and prophesying often became a regular part of their services.

In resigning from the Church of England and trying to separate their churches from all contact with worldly corruption, Separatists in effect resigned one of the traditional responsibilities of the church, namely the propagation of the faith. In their attack on the Church of England they had to admit that its preachers had been the means of bringing faith to many, including themselves. But they denied that the preaching of the Word to unbelievers was a necessary characteristic of a true church, which by their definition was an association of men already converted. The preaching of their own ministers was designed for the existing members (to nourish and strengthen their existing faith), not for unregenerate men in need of spiritual awakening. When confronted with the fact that this left no means of spreading the gospel, they shifted the burden off on the state. The government, they suggested, might hire a number of speakers to preach appropriate sermons to the unconverted. If conversions resulted, the new believers could form churches of their own with genuine ministers.[23]

As long as other churches supplied them with a fund of members, most Separatists did not care to face the implications of their position. But other Puritans would not allow them to escape altogether. Separatism, it was pointed out again and again, depended for its converts on those very churches which it denounced as Antichristian: Separatists did no more than gather in the fruits of other men's preaching in the Church of England, and in doing so they belied their own condemnation of that church.

With a few Separatists the argument struck home. Among them was probably John Robinson, pastor of the Separatist church at Leyden which eventually sent the Pilgrims to Plymouth. Robinson decided that the English parish assemblies, if not quite churches, could not be totally outside the fellowship of Christ. Because of their promiscuous membership a true Christian could not join with them in the Lord's Supper. But their ministers did preach the Word, and even true Christians might profitably join with the unregenerate in hearing it. "The hearing of the Word of God," said Robinson, "is not so inclosed by any hedge, or ditch, divine or human, made about it, but lies in common for all, for the good of all." [24] The Lord's Supper, on the other hand, was not for the good of all. A hedge must close it to the unregenerate. Robinson thus accepted the distinction by which non-separating Puritan ministers maintained their precarious balance between ideal and reality: all might participate in hearing the Word, but the Lord's Supper ought to be reserved for the faithful, who were joined in the bond of the Spirit. "So," Robinson declared,

when there come into the church assembly, unbelievers, heathens, Turks, Jews, atheists, excommunicants, men of all religions, men of none at all, and there hear, 1 Cor. xiv. 23, what spiritual communion have they with the church . . . or one with another . . . ? Hearing simply, is not appointed of God to be a mark and note, either of union in the same faith, or order amongst all that hear, or of differencing of Christians from no Christians; or of members from no members of the church: as the sacraments are notes of both in the participants.[25]

Robinson was not persuaded to return to the Church of England, but he was ready to hear its preachers and even to join in private prayer with Christians who remained within it.

Robinson's position was an uncomfortable stopping place because it skirted the crucial question of whether the parish assemblies of England were true churches. Robinson implied that they performed properly some of the functions of churches, but he was obliged to deny that they were in fact true churches. Otherwise there could be no excuse for separating from them. The non-separating Puritans, on the other hand, held an even more difficult position. They affirmed that the parish assemblies were true churches, but they were obliged to admit that wicked men could freely take the Lord's Supper in them.

The New World, along with its other attractions, offered non-separating Puritans a way out of this dilemma. Here they could affirm their loyalty to the church that bred them and at the same time form churches of their own in which all comers might hear the Word but only the godly would take the sacraments. After 1630 they flocked by the thousands to Massachusetts, Connecticut, and New Haven and established churches that resembled closely the Separatist one already functioning at Plymouth. Indeed, they outdid the Separatists in the standards of holiness demanded of members.[26]

To this haven in 1631 came Roger Williams. He was welcomed by the other Englishmen there, for his reputation as an eloquent, learned, and earnest preacher of the Word had preceded him. Nearly all the settlers struggling through their first New England winter were Puritans. And if few of them were Separatists, they had found the Separatists at Plymouth much to their liking. If they had heard that Roger Williams was a Separatist, it may not initially have disturbed them. He was an Englishman and a Puritan. If he was a Separatist like the people at Plymouth that fact need not come between them. The church just established at Boston was badly in need of someone to fill the place of its pastor, John Wilson, who was to leave for England on the return voyage of the ship that had brought Williams. Wilson, everyone hoped, would be returning shortly, but Atlantic voyages were perilous, and so was life for a Puritan in Charles I's England. Besides, a church should properly have two ministers, a pastor and a teacher. The Boston church liked Roger Williams—nearly everyone who ever encountered him did—and they promptly offered him the post of teacher.

The young man—Williams was under thirty—gave an ominous response. After talking with the members of the church, he declined the offer, because, as he later reported, "I durst not officiate to an unseparated people, as, upon examination and conference, I found them to be." [27] Williams' meaning is underlined in John Winthrop's contemporary account of the episode. Williams, Winthrop says, "refused to join with the congregation at Boston, because they would not make a public declaration of their repentance for having communion with the churches of England, while they lived there." [28]

Williams, it began to appear, was a special kind of Separatist. Though he had come to a place where Puritans could enjoy the advantages of separation without separating, he was not prepared to share in a geographical evasion of the issue. Christians must not merely leave the Church of England, they must denounce it. He refused to join the Boston church, not because it exhibited any faults of its own (it was congregational in practice, based on a covenant, had church discipline and regenerate membership), but because the Bostonians would not indulge in public remorse for having ever had anything to do with the non-Church of England.

Being a Separatist meant for Williams, among other things, a constant alertness to avoid even the most tenuous connection with the church to which he once belonged. A public statement of the kind he wanted would have invited an investigation by the English government, with probable revocation of the charter that made Puritan Massachusetts possible. But Roger Williams had not crossed the ocean to compromise. In this land of new beginnings and opportunities he was bent on bringing God's true religion into pure and proper practice. After refusing Boston, he went to Salem, where some church members may already have expressed Separatist convictions; but before he could conclude his examination of the people there or they of him, the authorities in Boston warned them against him.[29] Williams then went off to the avowedly Separatist church at Plymouth, becoming a member and assistant to the pastor. But the difference between his Separatism and that practiced at Plymouth became clear when some members of the church paid a visit to England, attended church services there, and went unrebuked for it upon their return. The Plymouth church evidently followed or at least condoned the position of its former pastor in Leyden, John Robinson. Williams would have none of it. Not only was it wrong to hear Anglican preachers, but it was wrong to remain a member of a church that failed to censure or excommunicate members who did so.[30]

Williams returned to Salem in 1633 and became teacher of the church there in 1635, presumably after satisfying himself that the members had made some proper expression of remorse for their former connection with the Church of England; he later declared that the church "was known to profess separation." [31] The question that troubled him at Plymouth probably did not arise at first, but it evidently did before long, for shortly after his exile to Rhode Island, Winthrop recorded that Williams "had so far prevailed at Salem as many there (especially of devout women) did embrace his opinions, and separated from the churches [of Massachusetts], for this Cause, that some of their members, going into England, did hear the ministers there, and when they came home the churches here held communion with them." [32]

This hypersensitivity to contact with the Church of England was only one of the ways in which Williams tried the patience of the other settlers of New England. At Salem he broached a succession of opinions that seemed to many to have nothing but novelty to commend them. He thought the settlers' title to the land was invalid because derived from the King of England, whose claim to it, Williams had decided, was fraudulent. He thought the government had no authority to punish breaches of the first four commandments (the first table) of the Decalogue. He thought the government should not impose an oath of loyalty. He thought a man should not pray with his wife unless both were regenerate.[33]

In these opinions the direction of Williams' intellectual growth is revealed. To his contemporaries they seemed eccentric, not to say criminal, and because of them he was banished from Massachusetts. But they were all rooted, as will become apparent, in the ideas he had learned as an Englishman, a Puritan, and a Separatist. And they point ahead to the intricate, almost systematic set of ideas about church and state that inspired his later writings.

II

The Church and Its Ministry

Roger Williams left England because he thought the Church of England was wrong. He left Massachusetts, though not quite voluntarily, because he thought the churches of Massachusetts were wrong. Most of his writings were demonstrations that other people were wrong. Yet he was not a quarrelsome man. His successive separations were acts not so much of defiance as of discovery, a progression through the wilderness toward the church. Throughout his writings the most persistent image was that of the church as a garden, in which Christ separated His saints from the world. Within this garden all must be holy. The exclusion of every worldly weed was not simply an obligation but a necessity. A bed of weeds was no garden.[1]

The Equality of Worship

For Williams the distinction between church and world obliterated any other distinction that came up against it. Other Puritans, though they earned their name by seeking to protect the church from worldly corruption, nevertheless allowed the church some responsibility for the sinners surrounding it. They were willing to recognize as in some sense converted to Christianity men who understood and believed Christian doctrine, but who had not yet undergone the "conversion" that brought saving grace. Williams refused any such extension of meaning. Only a man who had experienced grace was converted. Only such a man was a Christian.[2]

Williams was particularly incensed by the word "Christendom," which seemed to imply that the inhabitants of a country professing belief in Christianity were truly Christians. The mass of men in this "most unchristian Christendome," despite their baptism and attendance on the rites of the church, were not Christians and must not be so named.[3] "Christenings make not Christians" was his comment on missionary efforts that deluded the heathen into thinking that God could become theirs by the singing of psalms, the saying of prayers, and the sprinkling of water.[4] Words like "Christian" and "church" could be instruments of perdition when they were stretched to include any part of the world save God's elect.

By the same token, Williams refused to recognize distinctions within the church, whether between members or between acts of worship. The difference between church and world was absolute, the one pure, the other impure, and the purity of the church did not admit of degrees.

There could not be one part of church worship that was more pure than others. The trouble with the non-separating Puritans as with Separatist John Robinson was that, in the effort to straddle church and world, they manufactured a distinction of their own and failed to recognize that it violated the supremacy of the distinction between church and world. To allow church members to hear preaching in the Church of England but not to take the Lord's Supper there was to walk in a no man's land between Christ and Antichrist, between the church and the world, between the garden and the wilderness. The worship of God in the church of Christ was not divisible into essential and non-essential. There was no middle ground between sacred and profane.

Williams believed that the preaching of the Word, both for him who did the preaching and for those who heard him, was no less holy than any other part of the church service. He probably argued the point first in a tract against John Robinson, written in 1637, which has not survived.[5] Later, in *The Bloudy Tenent* he explained that "teaching and being taught in a Church estate is a Church worship, as true and proper a Church worship as the Supper of the Lord." [6] And every part of church worship was sacred. "Since," he challenged his opponents, "you both seem to magnifie the Seales of Baptisme and the Lords Supper with a difference and excellency above other Ordinances, We Querie where the Lord Jesus appointed such a difference and distinction? And whether there was not as full Communion practised by the first Christians in the Word, Prayer, and Communitie, as in the breaking of Bread?" [7] Other Separatists who had not gone over to Robinson's position agreed with Williams in repudiating the distinction.[8] But in his exploration of what that repudiation implied, Williams went far beyond them and transformed it into a positive, controlling principle of ecclesiastical theory. Within the church, Williams believed, all acts of worship were created equal. All were holy, and Christians must not share any of them with non-Christians, because God would withhold His presence from any group of worshippers that knowingly included wicked men. To be sure, Christians, although endowed with a measure of sanctity by God's saving grace, were nevertheless men, and while in the world they must do the business of the world with other men. But when worshipping God in the church or out of it they must be utterly separate.

The uncompromising application of this principle accounts for some of the seemingly eccentric views that Williams allegedly uttered while in Massachusetts, for example, that "a man ought not to pray with such [the unregenerate], though wife, child, etc." [9] It was wrong by Williams' reasoning for the godly ever to join in prayer with the ungodly; and since a family would usually contain both, family prayers in most homes would be wrong.

Williams also objected to the colony's requirement of a loyalty oath from all its inhabitants, because an oath, invoking the name of God, was an act of worship. As such it must be reserved for the regenerate; a magistrate "ought not to tender an oath to an unregenerate man." [10] Williams later discussed the subject in *The Hireling Ministry None of Christs*, affirming that it was lawful "for Christians to invocate the Name of the most High in Swearing." But since an oath was "a part of his holy worship, and sometimes put for his whole worship," it was proper only "unto such as are his true Worshippers in Spirit and Truth." And as he had opposed the loyalty oath in Massachusetts, so he raised in Cromwell's England the question "Whether the inforcing of Oaths and spirituall Covenants upon a Nation promiscuously, and the constant inforcing of all persons to practice this Worship in the most triviall and common cases in all Courts (together with the Ceremonies of Booke, and holding up the hand etc.) be not a prostituting of the Holy Name of the most High to every unclean Lip." [11] When a Christian magistrate administered an oath to an unregenerate man, he was guilty of prostituting the Holy Name; he was an accomplice, as guilty as the oath taker in profaning a sacred act, as guilty as the Christian who prayed with his unregenerate wife.

While Williams was in Massachusetts, he became increasingly convinced that a church was imperfectly separated from the world if it allowed its members to join with unregenerate men in any act of worship, whether oath, prayer, or simply being taught by a preacher. He had probably also begun to feel what he later insisted on, that for Christians to mingle with unbelievers in worship was not merely corrupting to the believers but unfair to the unbelievers. An act of worship, though a means of grace for believers (when properly performed in separation from the world), was an act of sin for unbelievers. Like the followers of Jonathan Edwards a century and more later, Williams thought it compounded the wickedness of wicked men when they went through the motions of religion: "whatever such an unbelieving and unregenerate person acts in Worship or Religion, it is but sinne, Rom. 14. Preaching sinne, praying (though without beads or booke) sinne; breaking of bread, or Lords supper sinne." [12] For regenerate men to participate with unbelievers in the latters' pretended worship was thus to encourage them in sin and at the same time to hide from them the awful condition in which they stood. By being allowed to participate in acts that properly belonged only to believers, the unregenerate were lulled into security: "the misapplication of Ordinances [i.e., preaching, prayer, or the sacraments] to unregenerate and unrepentant persons hardens up their soules in a dreadfull sleep and dreame of their owne blessed estate, and sends millions of soules to hell in a secure expectation of a false salvation." [13]

As Williams saw it, the government of Massachusetts was guilty of fostering this kind of deception when it required all persons, church members or not, to attend services, even though the sacraments were reserved for members. To compel the unregenerate to hear the preaching of the Word in church was to bring the world into the church, to compel both the regenerate and the unregenerate to sin, the latter in going through one of the motions of worship, the former in joining them. The same thing was wrong with compulsory church attendance of unbelievers in Massachusetts that was wrong with the voluntary attendance of believers at the preaching of English ministers in the Church of England. In both cases an invalid distinction was made between the sacraments and other acts of worship. The worship of God was a seamless fabric. No part of it could be separated from the rest, and every part must be kept separate from the world.

Full Repentance and Full Separation

In affirming the equality of all acts of worship, Williams was in effect demanding a stricter standard of participation in the church. The non-separating Puritans in England had argued that only the elect, only those who could detect the motions of grace in their souls, should presume to take Communion. Williams was arguing that only such persons should be allowed to attend church services at all. Not surprisingly his zeal for exclusion of the ungodly led him to approve a new qualification for church membership that came to be applied in Massachusetts some time after his arrival. Before the founding of Massachusetts, congregationalism had been practiced mainly in Separatist churches, which seem to have taken a candidate's presumption of grace along with godly behavior and a formal profession of faith as evidence of regeneration sufficient for admission to the church. During the first two or three years of the Bay Colony's existence the same procedure was probably followed in the new churches there. But sometime around 1633 the Massachusetts churches began requiring every candidate for admission to demonstrate his regeneration by narrating the spiritual experiences in which he had detected the presence of saving grace within himself. He was expected to be familiar with the morphology of conversion as taught by Puritan ministers; and in order to convince the other members of his worthiness to join the church, he had to explain his passage through the various stages, up through the crucial one in which conviction of sin was followed by the stirrings of grace. Williams probably did not share in any important way in the establishment of this requirement, which seems to have been developed out of the non-separating tradition of emphasizing that only those who had felt saving grace should take the sacrament.[14] Although Williams repudiated any distinction among acts of worship, he could still wholeheartedly approve of the new test as a worthwhile refinement of admissions practices. It was a way of keeping out worldlings—whether honest men mistaken about their regeneration or outright hypocrites—who might otherwise slip into the church undetected.

At the time when Williams debated with the Quakers in 1672, he praised the test as "that gallant and heavenly and fundamental Principle of the true matter of a Christian Congregation, Flock or Society, viz. Actual Believers, true

Disciples and Converts Living Stones, such as can give some account how the Grace of God hath appeared unto them, and wrought that Heavenly Change in them." In the margin he wrote, "This was and I hope is the principle of the N. English Church." [15] But, for Williams, the new test was not enough. And he proceeded to devise still another requirement for admission to church membership, this one coming directly out of Separatist tradition.

In the preceding chapter it was suggested that the mere willingness to leave the Church of England probably constituted an implicit renunciation of its validity as a church, and one early Separatist church covenant had included a statement in which candidates explicitly renounced the Church of England and promised not to return to its corruptions.[16] Being non-Separatists the Massachusetts Puritans made no such renunciation, explicit or implicit, in their church covenants, but they did demand that candidates show specific proof of regeneration. Williams, accepting the Massachusetts requirement, went on to distinguish between godly persons (who could pass the Massachusetts test) and such godly persons who had also perceived and fully repented for their sin in having formerly practiced false worship in the Anglican non-church. Although the process of regeneration as described in Puritan writings required humiliation, conviction of sin, and repentance for former and continuing sins, it was possible, Williams believed, to go through these steps and to receive saving grace without recognizing the enormous sin of having performed idolatrous acts of false worship in an Antichristian church. Only after a regenerate man had come to such a recognition and had professed his repentance, before man and God, was he proper material for church membership. No Puritan minister would admit a former whore to church fellowship, said Williams, "without

sound Repentance for the filthines of her skirts (Lament.
1.) not only in actuall whoredomes, but also in whorish
Speeches, Gestures, Appearances, Provocation. And why
should there be a greater strictnes for the skirts of common
whoredom, then of spiritual and soul Whoredome, against
the chastitie of Gods Worship?" [17]

This repentance was of itself an important religious
experience, and might even come to a believer as a sort of
second regeneration. "And this is the reason," Williams
wrote in 1644,

why although I confesse with joy the care of the New
English Churches, that no person be received to Fellowship
with them, in whom they cannot first discerne true Re-
generation, and the life of Jesus: yet I said and still affirm,
that godlie and regenerate persons (according to all the
former instances and reasons) are not fitted to constitute
the true Christian Church, untill it hath pleased God to
convince their soules of the evill of the false Church, Minis-
try, Worship, etc. And although I confesse that godly persons
are not dead but living Trees, not dead, but living Stones,
and need no new Regeneration (and so in that respect need
no felling nor digging out) yet need they a mighty worke
of Gods Spirit to humble and ashame them, and to cause
them to loath themselves for their Abominations or stincks
in Gods nostrils (as it pleaseth Gods Spirit to speak of false
Worships:) Hence Ezek. 43. 11. Gods people are not fit for
Gods House, untill holy shame be wrought in them, for
what they have done. Hence God promiseth to cause them
to loath themselves, because they have broken him with
their whorish hearts, Ezek. 6. 9. And hence it is that I have
known some precious godly hearts confesse, that the pluck-
ing of their souls out from the Abominations of false
worship, hath been a second kind of Regeneration.[18]

Given Williams' position that all acts of worship were equal and that all must be performed only by believers and only in separation, it was easy enough to find convincing proof that not all regenerate persons were qualified for church membership. Martin Luther was his favorite example: "How did famous Luther himself continue a Monk, set forth the German Masse, acknowledge the Pope, and held other grosse abominations concerning Gods worship, notwithstanding the life of Christ Jesus in him, and wrought in thousands by his means." Luther, in other words, though regenerate, had performed various acts of worship falsely and wickedly. He would therefore not have been worthy of membership in a rightly constituted, truly separated Christian church, had any existed in his lifetime.[19]

The same was true of the martyrs burned by Queen Mary. Separatists had always contended that the presence in the Church of England of some regenerate members was not a sufficient reason to consider it a church. Williams added that regeneration was not enough to make even a church member, let alone a church. When John Cotton argued that all godly, that is regenerate, persons were fit for membership, Williams pointed out that Cotton himself demanded more than that from candidates, for, since coming to Massachusetts, he had refused "to receive persons eminent for personal grace and godlinesse, to the Lords Supper, and other privileges of Christians (according to the profession of their Church estate) until they be convinced of the necessity of making and entering into a Church covenant with them, with a confession of faith, etc. and if any cannot bee perswaded of such a covenant and confession (notwithstanding their godlinesse, yet) are they not admitted." [20] The qualifications for admission demanded by Cotton (and by Massachusetts) were all right as far as they went. But in addition, Williams insisted, a candidate must show full repentance for the great sin of false worship that he might not have recognized as a sin at the time of his regeneration.

How far Williams pressed his call for separation from the Church of England before he left Massachusetts is not clear. It had carried him from Boston to Salem to Plymouth and back to Salem again, and it may also have been behind his demand in 1635 that the Salem church renounce the other churches of Massachusetts. Although the demand could have been occasioned simply by the intervention of the other churches in the Salem church's contest with the Massachusetts government, Williams was perhaps even then applying the logic that later made him condemn the Massachusetts churches as all tainted with Roman corruption (indeed "still fastned to the Pope himself") because of their refusal to renounce and repent of their connection with the similarly tainted English churches.[21]

During his years in Massachusetts, Williams was riding the crest of an intellectual wave that was sweeping both him and the Puritans who disagreed with him toward new heights of church purity. He was very sensitive to the rapid progress in this direction that he and his generation had made. He never tired of reminding John Cotton of the numerous advances that Cotton himself had made on the way from the Church of England to the New England practices.[22] Williams' own efforts to keep weeds out of God's garden had led him to prescribe conditions for church membership that went farther than the Separatists had gone in England, Holland, or Plymouth, and farther than the non-separating Puritans in either old or New England. His awareness of how radically he and others had changed their views kept him looking for still more advances, and not long after arriving in Rhode Island he did have some new thoughts about the qualifications of church members.

Hitherto, like other Puritans, including the Separatists,

he had accepted the validity of his baptism, though performed by a minister of the Church of England. It was
standard Puritan doctrine that baptism, not only in the
Church of England but even in the Roman Catholic Church,
was valid and need not be repeated. But if all parts of church
worship were equal, and if the Church of England was a
false church, then that church's baptism was false (and had
always been). By 1644 Williams was drawing this conclusion
in print,[23] and if we may believe the reports that John Winthrop heard from Rhode Island in 1638, Williams already
by that time had come to reject the validity of his baptism.
Presumably Williams rejected it either because it was performed in a false church or else because it was performed
in infancy. The latter was the position taken by the Ana-
baptists, who maintained that baptism, being a sacrament,
must be reserved, equally with the Lord's Supper, for com-
prehending, regenerate adults. It was the Anabaptist position that Winthrop attributed to Williams. Winthrop recorded in 1639 that "a sister of Mrs. [Anne] Hutchinson
[who, banished from Massachusetts, had just gone to Rhode
Island], the wife of one Scott, being infected with Ana-
baptistry, and going last year to live at Providence, Mr.
Williams was taken (or rather emboldened) by her to make
open profession thereof, and accordingly was rebaptized by
one Holyman, a poor man late of Salem. Then Mr. Williams
rebaptized him and some ten more. They also denied the
baptizing of infants, and would have no magistrates." [24]
    Shortly thereafter, Winthrop confirmed and amplified
the report, saying that "Mr. Williams and many of his company, a few months since, were in all haste rebaptized, and
denied communion with all others." [25] Although Williams
nowhere discusses his views of infant baptism, Winthrop's
report was plausible, even probable. But apparently even
this advance in church purity did not satisfy Williams for

long, and his next position, according to Winthrop, was to refuse to worship with anyone except his wife.

Winthrop's report may have exaggerated the extent of Williams' exclusiveness, but Williams had clearly pushed the principle of separation to the point where the church was threatened with extinction for lack of suitable members. At this point, however, his thinking about membership was brought to an impasse by another ecclesiastical problem that had been troubling him, the problem of the ministry and its relationship both to the church and to the God in whose name it acted. As he confronted this problem in its farthest reaches, his search for a pure church was perforce suspended. And for reasons that will become apparent, he never resumed it.

Apostles and Pastors

Williams' concern about the nature of the ministry and the means of its coming into existence evidently began, like his other concerns, before he left Massachusetts or perhaps even in England. In one later tract he indicated that part of his dispute with Cotton, presumably while still in the Bay Colony, "was concerning the true Ministery appointed by the Lord Jesus," and that "Another was concerning the fitnesse and qualification of such persons as have right (according to the rules of the Gospel) to choose and enjoy such a true Ministery of the Lord Jesus." [26] And given the trend of Williams' thought, it would have been hard for him to escape a dispute on these subjects.

In a properly constituted church, as all congregational Puritans agreed, the members who were joined in covenant had the right to choose and install their own minister. In electing him to office they called him to separate himself from the world and serve them in the worship of God. It was his calling, Williams believed, to lead and feed them and them only; his sermons must therefore be directed to them and them only. The sermons of ministers in Separatist churches were doubtless so directed and, according to Williams, so were those of the orthodox New England clergy.[27] But Williams made explicit an implication that other Puritans, Separatist and non-Separatist, preferred to ignore: he flatly stated that it was wrong of a minister to present his church with a sermon designed for conversion. "Now then that man that professeth to feed a Flock or Church, with the Ordinances of Word and Prayer, he must needs acknowledge that his proper worke is not to preach for conversion, which is most preposterous among a converted Christian people . . . the Pastors worke is to feed his Flock, Acts. 20. and prophecie is not for unbe[li]evers, but for them that beleeve, to edefie, exhort and comfort the Church, I Cor. 14.3. 22." [28]

Williams gave few hints as to precisely how he thought preaching to feed souls should differ from preaching to convert unbelievers and prepare them for church membership. But he evidently thought that the two were incompatible, because the purposes differed so vitally. The unbeliever must obviously be taught the elements of Christian doctrine and must arrive at a conviction of and repentance for his own great sinfulness. And before he became fit to join a church, he must also achieve that special repentance (from false worship formerly practiced) that Williams again and again stressed as an essential qualification for church membership. Most of such teaching would be superfluous to church members, who needed more advanced instruction, and would thus be inappropriate in a minister's regular sermons. The minister's obligation was to the men who elected him, not to the world at large.

Williams once admitted that an unbeliever, if he happened to hear a pastor's preaching, might be converted by it; but, he said, "this is accidentall that any unbeleever should come in." [29] Accidental it must be because in a proper church only members would ordinarily be present at worship. And by Williams' view the accident would be more likely to sink the unbeliever deeper in sin than to convert him: by hearing himself addressed as though he were one of the saints he sat amongst instead of the wretched sinner he actually was, the stranger might be flattered into a perilous security. In any case, sermons designed for church members could contain little that was helpful, comprehensible, or even pertinent to an unregenerate man.

Paradoxically, at the same time that Williams forbade ministers to preach for conversion, he accepted the standard Puritan view that conversion normally came to a sinner or infidel only after instruction through the preaching of the Word. Puritans, searching their souls in order to test the truth or falsity of their conversions, asked themselves whether their feelings of humiliation, conviction, and assurance had been preceded by the preaching of the Word. And any applicant for membership in a Massachusetts church whose alleged conversion had not included this step would doubtless have been rejected. A conversion not generated by preaching would have been considered illusory. Williams himself dismissed the validity of Quaker conversions because they did not follow this pattern. [30]

The question thus arose for Williams, if conversion must be preceded by preaching, and if ministers must preach only to the converted, how is the circle to be broken? Where can converts be found to begin any new church or continue an old one? Orthodox Puritans, who felt no compunction about worshipping in a mixed congregation, could answer that ministers converted the unbelievers at the same time as they nourished the faith of those already converted. John Cotton, for example, saw no reason why the same sermon should not do double duty for believers and unbelievers. "And what is preaching the word," asked Cotton, "but explication and application of it? and is not the explication and application of the word, as fit to feed soules, as to convert them?" [31] Williams thought not. His conception of church purity and of the minister's relation to his church precluded pastoral preaching as a source of converts. The only proper instrument for bringing men to Christ, he believed, must be a special apostolic type of minister whose calling was to preach a special kind of sermon to the unconverted. As they became converted he would gather them into churches to be presided over by pastors and teachers. The apostles and evangelists commissioned by Christ had been ministers of this kind; and though some of them had also ministered to regular churches, they had taken pains not to confound the two functions. When an apostle preached to unbelievers, he evidently did not preach to them in the way he did to believers, and he did not join with them in prayer or other acts of worship lest they be deluded into thinking themselves fit for communication with the Lord. [32]

Williams longed to undertake an apostolic ministry himself. Shortly after he came to New England, he told John Winthrop that he did not wish to be an elder (i.e., a pastor or teacher) in any church "if the Lord please to grant my desires that I may intend what I long after, the natives souls. . . ." [33] Probably with this end in mind, while he was living at Plymouth and Salem he labored to learn the language of the Indians, lodging with them, as he later remembered "in their filthy smoky holes." When he went to Rhode Island, at Winthrop's suggestion, it was because "My souls desire was to do the natives good . . . and therefore desired not to be troubled with English company." [34] Williams' first publication, *A Key into the Language of America* (1643), gave abundant evidence of the time he had spent among them. No New Englander burned with more evangelical zeal. If he could have persuaded himself that it was religiously, ecclesiastically, and historically possible to become an apostle, whether among the Indians or anywhere else, he would surely have done so.

Apparently there was a time, in 1639, when he had some expectation of undertaking such an office. In that year, shortly after he and his followers had undergone rebaptism, as Winthrop reported, Williams began to question his second baptism, this time on the ground that he could not "derive the authority of it from the apostles, otherwise than by the ministers of England, (whom he judged to be ill authority,) so as he conceived God would raise up some apostolic power. Therefore he bent himself that way, expecting (as was supposed) to become an apostle; and having, a little before, refused communion with all, save his own wife, now he would preach to and pray with all comers." [35]

In this brief passage Winthrop recorded Williams' entry upon a line of thought that was to shape the remainder of his life. The details of Winthrop's report may be erroneous. Probably even at this early stage Williams would have refrained from praying with all comers. What seems indisputable is that he wished to practice the apostolic ministry. But when he looked for authority to undertake it, when he searched the Scriptures and the history of the church to see how one went about it, he came upon an insurmountable barrier. The only ministry recognized by congregational Puritans, whether Separatist or non-Separatist, was that of pastors and teachers elected by a congregation. Williams could find no authorization for a church to elect apostles to spread the gospel. The original apostles and evangelists had been commissioned by Christ himself. He had endowed them with powers to appoint others, to continue the succession in a chain, so that each might trace his commission directly back to Christ. An apostolic minister, indeed any minister, must be commissioned either by Christ himself or by another duly authorized minister, whose authority came originally from Christ. But alas for Williams: he could not make himself believe that anyone in his world enjoyed such a commission.

The Extinction of the Church

There was nothing particularly novel in thinking that ministers were of two kinds, apostolic and pastoral, and that a church could be gathered only by one of the apostolic kind. Both ideas were widely held in Williams' time and before. But they were not widely held by people who also believed, as Williams did, that Antichrist had overtaken the world in the person of the pope. And they were held by even fewer persons who believed that Antichrist had completely extinguished the ministry established by Christ. In adopting this combination of ideas Williams parted from both the Separatists and the non-separating Puritans. He had followed to its ultimate conclusion their view that a pastoral minister bore a relation only to the church that chose him. And he had gone on from there to a position that they wholly denied, namely that the preaching of an apostolic minister must precede the formation of any church; and to this he joined the equally unacceptable view that Antichrist had destroyed every previously existing ministry.

With his customary addiction to pursuing ideas to their conclusions, Williams could not be content with an Antichrist who was less than totally successful, and his scholarly investigations produced no evidence to allow him to think otherwise. Sometime after the reign of Constantine in the fourth century, he believed, Antichrist had snuffed out the ministry that Christ had planted and Christians had cherished through three or more centuries. Those who now claimed a line of succession through the apostles were "forced to run into the tents of Antichrist, and to plead Succession from Rome," and it was inconceivable to Williams that Christ's commission could be delivered through Antichrist.[36] Until Christ came again and renewed the succession, there was no way left on earth to commission apostolic ministers who could gather true Christian churches. There neither was nor could be a church or a minister, apostolic or pastoral, in England or America or anywhere else in the world in the existing phase of human history. "In the poor small span of my Life," he wrote in 1652,

I desired to have been a diligent and Constant Observer, and have been my selfe many ways engaged in City, in Countrey, in Court, in Schools, in Universities, in Churches, in Old and New-England, and yet cannot in the holy presence of God bring in the Result of a satisfying discovery, that either the Begetting Ministry of the Apostles or Messengers to the Nations, or the Feeding and Nourishing Ministry of Pastors and Teachers, according to the first Institution of the Lord Jesus, are yet restored and extant.[37]

It was a position that Separatists and non-separating Puritans alike found absurd and shocking. All Protestants agreed that Antichrist had dominated the world for a length of time (which they thought to be drawing to a close), but most of them believed that Christ's visible church and ministry had existed throughout that time in some form, however imperfect.[38] And even if church and ministry had been extinguished in time past, it did not follow that they were still extinct. For most Puritans, and especially congregational Puritans, the gathering of a church did not involve apostolic succession. In both old England and New, Puritan ministers and theologians taught that the agreement of two or three (later seven) believers was a sufficient basis for starting a church.[39] Whatever spiritual power a church might have came not through apostolic succession, but directly from God upon the agreement of the initial members in a church covenant.

The church was thus a self-created organization, and as such it preceded the ministry in right and in time. Only election by a church could make a man a minister. Ordination, the ceremony through which the divine commission was thought to be handed on to a new minister in the Roman or Anglican church, was regarded by Puritans as a formality, not essential to the calling of a minister. William Perkins, before Roger Williams was born, maintained that the ordination of a minister by bishops or other ministers was not necessary. "If in Turkey, or America, or elsewhere," he said, "the Gospell should be received of men, by the counsell and persuasion of private persons, they shall not need to send into Europe for consecrated Ministers, but they have power to chuse their owne Ministers from within themselves." [40] John Robinson, the pastor of the Separatist church at Leyden, also expounded the view that the church makes the minister, not vice versa, and can even exist for a considerable period without choosing a minister. And he too suggested that if the natives of America, by reading the Scriptures, should convert themselves, they would have full power from God to form churches and place ministers over them.[41]

In practice, the first Massachusetts churches chose ministers who had already been ordained in England and at first avoided any renunciation of the ministerial calling thus formerly conferred. But within a short time the New Englanders were affirming that a minister could not exist apart from his church, that therefore a minister ordained by a bishop in England was no minister in Massachusetts (or elsewhere) unless called to the office by a particular church.[42] The members of that church, moreover, could ordain him, install him in office, without outside help. The assembled ministers of New England in the Cambridge Platform of 1648 pronounced their official view that "there may be the essence and being of a church without any officers" and that ordination was "nothing else, but the solemn putting of a man into his place and office in the Church wher-unto he had right before by election, being like the installing of a magistrat in the common wealth."[43] The ceremony of ordination in a congregational church consisted in a "laying on of hands." The Cambridge Platform went on to affirm that this ceremony could be performed entirely by laymen: "In such Churches where there are no Elders, Imposition of hands may be performed by some of the Brethren orderly chosen by the church therunto. For if the people may elect officers which is the greater, and wherin the substance of the Office consists, they may much more (occasion and need so requiring) impose hands in ordination, which is the less, and but the accomplishment of the other."[44] For orthodox New England Puritans, then, ministers were made by churches. The church depended on no minister, pastoral or apostolic, for its creation. It began simply with a covenant among believers.[45]

At one time Williams must have accepted these standard Puritan views on the origins of the church and the ministry and on their continuance through the reign of Antichrist. But somewhere in his search for church purity he had apparently been considering the proper consecration of the minister who must direct all worship, and here Williams' profound sense of the distance between God and man must have combined with his study of the Scriptures and of history to explode his orthodox assumptions. If Puritans were distinguished from Anglicans by a stronger sense of the distance between God and man, Williams was a Puritan Puritan, a step removed from the others in his vision of the awful gap. Where orthodox Puritans thought a church was self-generating, originating simply in a church covenant, Williams insisted that no group of Christians, however filled with saving grace and however united by covenant, was endowed with the spiritual powers necessary to bestow the ministerial office. This could be done only by God, operating through an appointed agent, as He had operated through the apostles and evangelists. No group of men could become a church or assume the powers of a church simply by agreeing among themselves to do so. A messenger of God must act first, to gather and espouse the people to Christ and thus make them a church. They could not act until they were acted upon.[46] And God did not now choose to act upon them. They could only wait patiently until Christ came again to commission new agents of God to start churches. Until then there could be no true church of Christ.

Williams reached this conclusion reluctantly and with no great certitude. He sometimes spoke of the need for his generation to search out a way of commissioning apostles, but he was never able to satisfy himself that such a way had been found. The device which earlier Separatists had suggested, that the government commission them, Williams dismissed out of hand.[47] When in 1652 the Puritan Parliament took up this notion, Williams wrote a pamphlet to dissuade them, pointing out that there were no apostolic ministers to send. "None that I know of professing Christ

Jesus these many hundred years," he said, "have been able to . . . prove such a Ministery extant, otherwise then by some (seemingly) Prudential Inventions, or the Power of the Sword. . . ." [48] The government, he was sure, did not have any spiritual power to delegate to the men it proposed to send out as apostles in Christ's name. Spiritual power must come from God. It was human presumption to expect that God would bestow such power on a man just because the government appointed him to be an apostle (or because a group of saints elected him to be their minister).

Prophets in Sackcloth

Although Williams believed that no apostolic or pastoral ministry and hence no true church of Christ existed or was possible, he did not conclude that all preaching of the gospel and all assemblies of worship must cease during the reign of Antichrist. Throughout this period, he thought, God had raised up "prophets in sackcloth" to lead His people through the wilderness. Such men needed no commission or any calling by a church; they acted from the Holy Spirit, and "no man ever did nor ever shall truly go forth to Convert the Nations, nor to Prophecy in the present state of Witnesses, against Antichrist, but by the gracious Inspiration and Instigation of the holy Spirit of God." [49] This was the origin of the Waldensians, the Lollards, the Hussites, as well as the Calvinists and Lutherans, the martyrs of sixteenth-century England, and the great numbers of men in Williams' own time who had been moved by what seemed to be a great outpouring of the Spirit.

Through this direct action of the Spirit, God's grace had continued to operate among men, but not, Williams em-

phasized, in such a way as to furnish anyone qualified to
found a true church of Christ. Prophets in sackcloth—and
he aspired to be one himself—might serve as a medium of
bringing saving grace to others and thus introduce men
into God's invisible church (the company of the elect, past,
present, and future). They might spread the gospel, un-
covering more and more of the great truths contained in
the Scriptures, the truths that Antichrist had so long hidden
from human sight by suppressing the Scriptures. They
might even prophesy and pray with assemblies of the elect
in worship. But they were not authorized to found particular, visible churches that could administer God's sacraments.[50] Indeed, they did not necessarily even understand
the form that a true church of Christ would have to take
and so could neither repent their former false worship nor
replace it with true, as witness once again Luther and
Calvin. Though "God hath stir'd up Witnesses to Prophecie
in Sackcloth against the Beast, during his 42 moneths
reigne: yet those Witnesses have in their Times, more or
lesse submitted to Antichrist, and his Church, Worship,
Ministrie, etc. and so consequently have been ignorant of
the true Christ, that is, Christ taken for the Church in the
true profession of that holy Way of Worship, which he
himselfe at first appointed." [51]

Even if Luther and Calvin could have gained full knowledge of the true worship, they could not thereby have been
empowered to practice it by gathering a church. The license
of an apostle must be explicitly conferred. Williams accordingly did not try to gather churches among the Indians.
He learned their language, instructed them, worked with
them, protected them against the rapacity of his countrymen, and continued to thirst after their souls. But he
discounted and disapproved of efforts to erect churches
among them. He thought that the number of Indian

converts to be expected must in any case remain small until the downfall of Antichrist approached, for so it was written in the Apocalypse—and on this even John Cotton agreed.[52]

It seems likely that Williams' doubts about the possibility of an apostolic ministry did not at first lead him to question the validity of the existing churches and their pastoral ministry, at least where the members both demonstrated their possession of saving grace and also repented their former false worship in the Church of England. He seems to have accepted a call to the ministry of the church at Salem in 1635 [53] and must at that time have considered it a true church and his own calling as valid. But there is some evidence that the extinction of the church was already agitating his mind when he arrived in Massachusetts. In a paper which the editors of the *Winthrop Papers* have assigned to the time when Williams refused to join the Boston church in 1631, Winthrop raised the question: "If Christs Churches were utterly nullified, and quite destroyed [by Antichrist], then I demande when they beganne againe and where? who beganne them? that we may knowe, by what right and power they did beginne them: for we have not heard of any newe Jo: Baptist, nor of any other newe waye from heaven, by which they have begunne the Churches a newe." [54]

Winthrop was using this argument as a *reductio ad absurdum:* he wished to show that the churches of Christ had been corrupted but not destroyed by Antichrist. But it was a part of Williams' intellectual courage—which must have made it alarming to argue with him—that he dared embrace the seeming absurdities to which his opponents reduced him. And as we have seen, he did embrace this particular absurdity during the years that followed. Precisely when is not clear, although Winthrop's report of affairs in

Providence in 1639, quoted above, suggests that Williams was close to it at that time. When he visited England in 1643–44, he may have found others who had reached the same position during the proliferation of religious ideas that was going on in England then. Or perhaps conversation with other searchers after truth stimulated him to a full articulation of ideas that were still new to the men he talked with. In any case, Robert Baillie, an unsympathetic Presbyterian observer, noted in June, 1644, that one Mr. Williams was causing a schism among the Independents (Congregationalists) by "denying any true church in the world, and will have every man to serve God by himself alone, without any church at all." Six weeks later Baillie wrote that "Sundrie of the Independent partie are stepped out of the Church, and follows my good acquaintance Mr. Roger Williams—who sayes, there is no church, no sacraments, no pastors, no church-officers, or ordinances in the world, nor has been since a few years after the Apostles." [55]

It may be that Williams thus became the first leader of a number of English Puritans who were shortly labelled "Seekers." But if so, he must have quickly cut himself loose from them; for while they shared his belief that all existing churches were false, they also seem to have adopted a variety of Socinian and Antinomian principles that would have been anathema to him.[56] What he could not cut loose from was the awful conclusion to which his ideas had led him and from which they offered no escape: Christians had lost their church, and there was no present way to recover it.

This, then, was the impasse that blocked Williams in his thinking on the subject of church membership and this the route by which he reached it. His originality, his capacity for pursuing every idea through all its implications, and his courage in accepting whatever he discovered the implications to be, however unpalatable, had brought him to a position which made his search for a purer church anachronistic. Until God again gave men a means of gathering a true church of Christ, it was fruitless to worry about the membership.

Williams never stopped believing that if a true church of Christ could exist, it would be the kind he envisaged, in which regenerate men would be separated out of the world. And he continued to think that the so-called churches of New England, although imperfectly separated, were close copies of the real thing.[57] He had no difficulty in accepting most of their practices as the ones which true visible churches would have to follow when Christ came again. But try as he might, he could not find that God had authorized these or any other gatherings for worship that now claimed the name of church. They were all the product of wishful thinking, human inventions all, and to read God into them was only another example of human presumption. God was not at the beck and call of any group of self-appointed saints who wished to call themselves a church. He did not stand by, waiting for men to make churches for Him. God was God and man was man, and when God was ready to summon man to worship in His church, He would do so. For the moment He suffered Antichrist to rule, and until He ordained otherwise, men must live and die without a church. Since God willed it, it must be good and right. "Blessed Truth," says Peace to Truth in *The Bloudy Tenent*, "this doctrine of a Ministry before the Church, is harsh and deep, yet most true, most sweet." [58]

Only a Williams could have found sweet a doctrine that frustrated his yearning to be an apostle and silenced his preaching in the pastoral ministry on which he had originally embarked. And even Williams did not have the heart to argue others into so devastating a conclusion. It is possible that in the initial excitement of formulating his ideas he drew some others after him, as Robert Baillie stated. And his arch-opponent John Cotton was surely not the only one to see and point out that the conclusion was inescapable. But though Williams' arguments often provide the logic for the conclusion, none of his voluminous publications and none of his surviving private letters were written for the purpose of persuading others that the church was dead. Indeed, he left behind no statement of his belief so direct as that which Baillie attributed to him. Whenever his headlong manner of writing brought him close to the subject, he pulled up short and changed directions. In his first controversial tract, in 1644, he mentioned, but only mentioned, the need "that in these great Earthquakes, wherein it pleaseth God to shake foundations, civill and spirituall, such a Ministry of Christ Jesus may be sought after, whose proper worke is preaching, for converting and gathering of true penitents to the fellowship of the Son of God." [59] Again in *The Bloudy Tenent,* when Peace raises the question, "Who then may rightly challenge that commission," that is, the commission to preach the Word and found churches, Truth answers, "Sweet Peace, in due place and season, that Question may be resolved." [60] A year later, in *Christenings make not Christians,* he came upon the question again, only to say, "I must ingenuously confesse the restlesse unsatisfiednesse of my soule in divers main particulars . . . in due place (haply) I may present such sad Queries to consideration. . . ." [61]

Williams had undergone so many transformations of opinion himself and had seen others do likewise in "these wonderful, searching, disputing and dissenting times" that he half expected to find some way out of his impasse. When his opponents accused him of denying the church altogether, he compared himself to one who suffers the night or an eclipse of the sun without denying the sun's existence.[62] He never urged men to stop worshipping God together; he kept discussing the proper form for the church as though it still existed; he even seemed to suggest that men should continue the search for a pure church and go through the motions of church worship while awaiting the return of Christ. But he could not conscientiously join with any group of worshippers who took upon themselves the name of a church.

Williams longed to think that his problem would shortly be solved by Christ himself. He was fond, like others of his time, of scrutinizing current events for signs of the impending advent. But he found little to encourage him. As he wrote to John Winthrop, Jr. in 1660, after Charles II had returned to the throne and the king of Spain was growing strong on New World treasures: "The Presbyterian party in England and Scotland is yet very likely to make some struggle against the Popish invasions; and yet in the end I fear (as long I have feared, and long since told Oliver, to which he inclined,) the bloody whore is not yet drunk enough with the blood of the saints and witnesses of Jesus." [63] And as the great event did not come, Williams never found the due place and season to press the sad queries that led him to doubt all churches and ministers.

The Offense of Quakerism

The only pretenders to church estate who received the full measure of Williams' skepticism were the Quakers. The disorganized, repetitious, tiresome, and sometimes eloquent diatribe which he published against them in 1676 is not to be read as an accurate statement of Quaker beliefs and practices but as a revelation of the outer dimensions of Williams' own beliefs and of the frustrations which his intellectual courage had brought to his life. Even the sarcasm of the title, *George Fox Digg'd out of his Burrowes* (Fox was the founder of Quakerism, Edward Burroughs his collaborator) hints at the unusual anger which this subject stirred in him. Williams in an earlier publication against John Cotton had noted that the non-separating Puritans suffered more heavily at the hands of the Anglicans than did the out-and-out Separatists, because "it is a principle in nature to preferre a professed enemie, before a pretended friend." [64] Something like this principle made Williams hate the Quakers. They looked for all the world like the prophets in sackcloth among whose number he counted himself. They appropriately claimed—though rather more ostentatiously than he—a direct calling from the Holy Spirit. And like him they professed to believe that the only present church was invisible. But instead of preaching the true gospel, they preached doctrines and indulged in practices that shocked Williams and other Puritans to the core; and instead of merely preaching, they gathered churches, or what amounted to churches, that defied every notion Williams had ever entertained of what a true church should be.

The source of the trouble, or perhaps merely a symptom of it, was the fact that the Quakers had a different interpretation of the Book of Revelation and thus a different view of history from the one professed either by Williams or by orthodox Puritans. The deciphering of Revelation was a complicated business, and there was wide disagreement among Protestant theologians about the signification of the various vials and seals and about the time scale involved. But the Quakers, according to Williams at least, reduced the prophecies of the book to a shambles by reading them as past rather than future. "The Quakers," he said, "though they hold Papists and Protestants (all except the Quakers) to be Anti-Christians . . . cast back all the

Prophesies of false Christs, false Prophets, and AntiChrist to the time of the Apostles themselves. . . ." [65]

In addition to excising the problem of Antichrist in this slashing manner, the Quakers misread history even more grievously in affirming that the second coming of Christ had already occurred and was occurring daily, because it was a spiritual, invisible coming, in the souls of true believers.[66] This easy solution to the problem of Christ's second coming evoked Williams' particular scorn. His sense of the gap between God and man had always saved him from reading divinity into his own or other men's aspirations. There was, besides, that streak of hardheaded realism in him, demanding visible, tangible, concrete evidence whenever human beings claimed contact with the Spirit—tests of faith, statements of repentance, observable saintly behavior. God dealt with man in terms of his earth-bound experience. The things of this world could be seen, felt, smelled, tasted. And when God had sent His son into the world, it was not as a spirit, not as an angel, whose ghostly presence must be sensed as an invisible light within. The Christ Williams knew about was a living, breathing, sweating, suffering Christ, whose presence in the world had been an indisputable fact. It was this visible Christ who had summoned His followers to worship God in visible churches. When He came again to the world, He would summon them again to visible churches. He would not conceal himself from the eyes of men. He would speak with the force of a trumpet and become again an indisputable, ascertainable fact.

Meanwhile only the deluded or wicked could indulge in the pretentious form of worship adopted by the Quakers. Had the Quakers been content to keep their inner light inner, devoting themselves in private to contemplation of its heavenly glow, Williams might have dismissed them as perhaps mistaken but harmless. But he could not forgive their *lèse majesté* in setting up visible assemblies for worship that were guided only by invisible inner light, when a visible historical Christ had come into the visible historical world and specifically laid down the only authentic rules for a visible worshipping church.

Yea, G. Fox and his Foxians, for all their being in God, and some of their proud and silly Answerings in Courts, that they live in God, and dwell in God, yet they disowne not their own visible Congregatings and Assemblings, their visible Teachers, Overseers, or Bishops, their visible and audible performances and Worships, praying, preaching, singing, etc. and why then doth this poor notoriously visible Cheatour thus prate of Invisibilities . . . ? [67]

When the Quakers entered the visible realm, they subjected themselves to visible standards; but instead of being guided by these standards, they ignored them. They ignored the Scriptures, holding that if every copy was lost, their own direct access to the Spirit would more than supply the lack. Instead of testing their inner light by the light of the Scriptures, they raised themselves above the Scriptures in inexcusable arrogance, making gods of themselves and taking their own whims for the movements of the Spirit. The churches of New England, to which Williams could not conscientiously join, at least grounded their actions on Christ's Word and tried to assure that their members should be regenerate. But "all that the Quakers Religion requires externally and internally to make Converts or Proselytes, amounts to no more then what a Reprobate may easily attain to and perform." [68] It was well known, according to Williams,

that if persons notoriously Deboist, come but to acknowledge a God and Christ within them, that is in English, that themselves are God and Christ, and can practice Thou and Thee, and Cheek by Joll with all their Betters, and can rail at and curse all that oppose them, and can come and bow down to a dumb Image and Worship without any great business of Contrition and Brokenness and Godly Sorrow, they are enroll and canonized for Saints and Gods etc. they are free from Sin, born of God and cannot sin, they now sit upon the twelve thrones and judge the unbelieving Jews and Gentiles in their heavenly places.

The wound lyes here (as it is with Papists, Arminians, and indeed with all mankind) in the soothing up and flattering of rotten Nature, from whence (from within the Lord Jesus tells us) proceed all the rotten and hellish Speeches and Actions.[69]

Because of the Quakers' deficient sense of the distance between man and God, they confused flesh and spirit, visible and invisible, church and world. And they failed to see the nature of their own humanity, a nature that could not be shed. Although Williams too was driven by a profound yearning for pure divinity, he would not allow himself to look beyond the world around him or through it. He looked straight at it and acknowledged what he saw: all men, including the regenerate, were corrupt at the core, irremediably so within this life; and all men, including the most separate Separatist, must live out their lives within this visible world, immersed in its corruption. The unpardonable sin of the Quakers was to think themselves out of it and out of their place in history.

If these poor filthy Dreamers lived without Food and Evacuations, without Physick (which some of them cry down, and no Physick but Faith) without Procreation, and bringing forth of Children without the filthiness and stinks

*of Nature; yea without the many thousands of Holy Words,
and Thoughts, and Actions omitted, and the many thousand
passionate, impertinent, unreasonable discontented Words
and Actions, etc. then might we say as the men of Iconium
(touching Paul and Barnabas) The Gods are come to us in
the likeness of Men, till then we must look upon the Foxians
(eating so Christ his flesh, etc. until they become Christ
himself,) as Simple, and Monstrous, and Blasphemous as
the Papists in their Foolish, Monstrous and Bloody Tran-
substantiations.*[70]

The church that Williams sought was a visible, tangible
church, that would exist in space and time, but separated,
so far as human ability permitted, from the rottenness,
corruption, and evil of the world. His church must be both
pure and visible, in the world but not of it, and founded
either by the Christ who had bled and died in the world
or by the one who would come to it again after the downfall
of Antichrist. Williams did not live to see such a church,
but he thought his New England neighbors to be close to
the form it must take, perhaps not as close as the Baptists
but much closer than the Quakers, who could not distinguish
between flesh and spirit.

The New Englanders were close enough to the ideal so
that Williams never urged them to give up, as he would
have liked to see the Quakers do. But even the New Englanders confused the church and the world. And the confusion was in some ways as bad for the world as it was for
the church. While Williams' reasoning led him to doubt
the present existence of the church, he was far from doubt-
ing the existence of the world; and his relentless differ-
entiation between the two led him to conclusions about the
world and its rulers that were as novel and daring as those
he reached about the church.

III

Church and State in Massachusetts

In thinking about the church, Williams took a number of accepted doctrines and pressed them to unaccepted conclusions. The same is true of his thinking about the state. Here again, however, it is impossible to appreciate the originality or even the meaning of his thought except by returning to his starting point in the ideas of the orthodox Puritans with whom he clashed. And nothing about the Puritans has been more widely misunderstood than their views of the relationship between church and state.

In the government of the United States, from the adoption of the Constitution to the present day, one of the outstanding characteristics of American freedom has been the strict separation of church and state. The Constitution originally made no mention either of religion or of God, and the First Amendment, adopted in 1791, took up the subject only to provide that "Congress shall make no law respecting an establishment of religion, or prohibiting the free exercise thereof." This provision has been pretty

rigorously adhered to. Not only the federal government but
the state governments too have generally followed the principle behind it, that church and state should be entirely
separate.

The government established in seventeenth-century
Massachusetts had no such reservations about its authority
in religious matters and did not hesitate to make laws respecting an establishment of religion. It allowed only church
members to vote, and it permitted no church to be gathered
without its approval. It provided for the support of the
ministry, and it punished anyone who spoke disrespectfully
of the ministers it supported. Precisely because the government of Massachusetts was so solicitous about the welfare
of the churches, later Americans have often assumed that
seventeenth-century New England stood at the opposite
pole from the strict separation of church and state sub-
sequently practiced in the United States. The government
of Massachusetts is frequently described as a theocracy, with
the implication that wide political powers rested in the
hands of the clergy. And the charge is supported by the fact
that Roger Williams indicted Massachusetts for mingling
church and state.

But Williams' indictment was not quite what it may seem
today, for seventeenth-century Massachusetts, so far from
presenting an identification of church and state, had made
a long step toward that separation which was to become the
American way. The step was not long enough to suit
Williams, but it was long enough to differentiate Massachusetts sharply from most of the rest of the world at the
time.

The Divine Right of Kings

The attitude of orthodox Puritans toward the relation of church and state had its origin in the political circumstances created by the Protestant Reformation. When Luther, Calvin, and their followers wished to escape the control of Rome, they could not hope to do so without the protection of a state that was willing to resist the forces which the papacy could bring to bear on them. Rome commanded the loyalty of Catholic monarchs, who might gladly undertake a conquest to maintain the faith and perhaps extend their own dominions at the same time. The papacy, moreover, although it had abandoned its ancient claim to direct control of civil rulers, was seeking to affirm an indirect control. Cardinal Bellarmine, the chief exponent of papal supremacy, affirmed that the pope, as spiritual leader of all Christians, could absolve the subjects of a heretical king from allegiance to him. Protestants, in support of any monarch who might support them, refurbished another ancient idea, that kings gained their authority directly from God and were not responsible to Rome in exercising it.[1]

In England King James himself became a principal spokesman for the Protestant position. In arguing for the divine right of kings, James asserted his own sovereignty over his subjects; but he asserted it *against* the pope. The king's authority, he maintained, came directly from God, and it did not travel by way of Rome. James's enthusiasm for royal power was unlimited, and by his reasoning a king's authority extended to spiritual as well as temporal matters. His Puritan subjects fully agreed that the king must protect *true* religion and that his commission to do so gave him supreme coercive powers in ecclesiastical matters, but they were careful to state the argument so as to retain the divine right of the church as well as the state. In the Puritan view, both church and state received authority directly from God, and both were charged with upholding His laws and worship. But though their duties thus overlapped, He had ordained them for different purposes and had endowed them with different powers. The state was concerned with the spiritual and temporal welfare of all the people within its bounds, and it was endowed with coercive temporal powers; the church was concerned solely with the spiritual welfare of its own members and was endowed with non-coercive spiritual powers. The state could employ armies and navies, constables and sheriffs, prisons and fines and bodily punishments, including the loss of life itself. The church could employ only argument, admonition, and ultimately excommunication, that is, expulsion from the fellowship of the godly. And even these weapons it must employ only in order to secure the repentance of the sinner, not to punish him.[2]

In supporting their rulers against papal interference, the Puritans stressed their belief that the church must not interfere with the state. If civil rulers received their authority directly from God, there was no need for the church to confirm the grant or to participate in its administration. And there was good reason why the church should not do so. The commission of the clergy, like that of rulers, was from God, but like Christ's commission from the Father, it did not extend to the things of this world: "Christ would not, must not goe beyond his Commission, received of the father. Now the Father gave him no such commission of a temporall Jurisdiction, no not so much as in small causes."[3] Whenever clergymen meddled in government, it was argued, they deserted the sacred role to which God had called them and slid toward the corruption and worldliness that had overtaken the Catholic Church.

Those Puritans who leaned toward congregationalism were particularly insistent that the church, because it was charged only with the spiritual welfare of its members (and of them only), must not become involved in the activities of the state, even when those activities were directed toward spiritual ends. The church must not do the state's work even at the state's request. Puritans hold, William Bradshaw wrote in 1605, "that no Ecclesiasticall Minister ought to exercise or accept of any Civill publique jurisdiction and authoritie, but ought to be wholly imployed in spirituall Offices and duties to that Congregation over which he is set. And that those Civill Magistrats weaken their owne Supremacy that shall suffer any Ecclesiasticall Pastor to exercise any civill jurisdiction within their Realmes, Dominions, or Seignories." To allow a clergyman to do the work of princes was to set him on the road to Rome: "the Pope is that Antichrist . . . because being but an Ecclesiastical officer he doth in the hight of the pride of his heart make claime unto, and usurp the Supremacy of Kings and civill Rulers of the Earth." [4]

With such views the Puritans could applaud King James for his attack on papal usurpation. But when they turned to examine his use of the authority for which he was contending, they found very little to applaud. England under James and Charles, as under Elizabeth before them, exhibited the awful spectacle of a church enmeshed in politics and a state that used the church in the administration of government. The king himself exemplified the very mixture of spiritual and temporal which he deplored in the pope, for the king of England was, ex officio, the head of the church in England. In Parliament the bishops and archbishops gave their voices in making laws; in their diocesan headquarters they presided over church courts that made their orders felt in every parish. Church courts exercised jurisdiction not only over moral offenses such as adultery but over many matters that had no direct connection with the salvation of souls. No one in England could inherit personal property until probate of the will had been granted in an ecclesiastical court. Puritans thought that marriage was a temporal matter; but in England only a clergyman could perform the ceremony, and church courts heard all cases involving disputes over marriage and divorce.[5]

Although the church courts maintained a pretense of dealing in spiritual penalties, the pretense was belied by the fees, amounting to fines in effect, collected at every stage in the hearing of a case and by the heavy civil disabilities arising from excommunication. An excommunicated person could not attend church, but might nevertheless be punished for not attending. Unless he humbled himself and obtained an absolution (for which another fee was collected), all Christians would be forbidden to communicate with him, a condition which might bring economic ruin. If he did not submit within forty days, the court could report him to the crown, and he would be imprisoned. Meanwhile he could not sue anyone in any court, civil or ecclesiastical, but he could be sued. And he could neither serve on a jury nor be a witness in any court.[6]

This blending of spiritual and temporal authority penetrated to the lowest level of public life: the parish served both church and state as the basic unit of administration. Church wardens, usually appointed locally to manage church property, were also involved in looking after paupers, discovering the fathers of bastard children, hiring schoolmasters, and a host of other civil matters. And yet they were responsible not to the state, but to the ecclesiastical courts.[7]

From the outset, the founders of New England were determined not to repeat these errors. Since their entire experience in public life hitherto had required participation in error, they were not well prepared to avoid it. It was sometimes necessary to make a mistake in order to recognize that it was a mistake. But they at least knew, from the works of theologians, what principles they must embody in their new institutions. It was of the first importance, they believed, that the clergy be denied any part in the civil government and that church discipline be conducted entirely by spiritual methods, without fines, fees, or imprisonment. That the state should not interfere with the exercise of discipline in any church was equally clear, but since the state must look after the spiritual as well as the temporal welfare of its subjects, godly rulers might easily be tempted to seek the assistance of the clergy and to draw them into the decisions and actions of government. John Winthrop saw the dangers involved more clearly than most of his colleagues, and it was under his guiding hand that Massachusetts gradually traced the dividing line between church and state—tortuous enough as Williams saw it, but surprisingly well marked when compared with the one drawn in England under James I or Charles I or their Puritan successors in the government.

The Massachusetts Way

The grossest evil of the English system was easily avoided in America. Neither Massachusetts nor any other English colony was subjected to the operations of an ecclesiastical court, because no member of the hierarchy with power to hold a court, no bishop or archdeacon, was ever located in America. The freedom from church courts in Massachusetts, however, was more than a mere default. The congregational system of church organization had its own method and its own officers of discipline. Although the non-separating

Puritans, while in England, had made less of discipline than
the Separatists, when they were free to erect churches of
their own in the New World, they were as strict as the
Separatists. Every church elected, besides a pastor and sometimes a teacher, one or more "ruling elders," lay officers
whose function was to keep watch over the daily behavior
of the members. Any member who encountered sinful conduct in another member was supposed to correct him, but
ruling elders were charged with discipline as their special
business. When an offender was spotted, unless his sin was
of a major order, like murder, rape, or adultery, the proper
procedure was to deal with him first in private. If this
produced no results, the case would be brought before the
whole church, which could formally admonish or censure
him, and if he remained obdurate excommunicate him.[8]

Thus the individual churches exercised the discipline
over moral and religious offenses that in England was
handled by ecclesiastical courts, but the worst that a church
could do to a man was excommunicate him. In Massachusetts, unlike England, this penalty was not a social and
economic catastrophe. Where only the proven elect were
entitled to membership in a church, excommunication
merely reduced a man to the status in which the majority
of the population found themselves anyhow.

The ineffectiveness of excommunication as a corrective
led the government of Massachusetts at one time to pass a
law on the subject. "Whereas it is found, by sad experience,"
the General Court declared, in September, 1638,

*that divers persons, who have bene justly cast out of some
of the churches, do prophanely contemne the same sacred
and dreadfull ordinance, by presenting themselves over-
bouldly in other assemblies, and speaking lightly of their
censures, to the great offence and greefe of Gods people,*

*and incuragment of evill minded persons to contemne the
said ordinance, it is therefore ordered, that whosoever shall
stand excommunicate for the space of 6 months, without
labouring what in him or her lyeth to bee restored, such
person shalbee presented to the Court of Assistants, and
there proceeded with by fine, imprisonment, banishment
or further. . . .*[9]

One man was indicted under this act, but before he could
be tried, the General Court came to its senses and repealed
the law, which mingled temporal and spiritual sanctions
and thus violated Puritan principle.[10] Two years later, in
1641, in order to make it plain that church discipline was
to have no civil consequences, the Court declared that "no
church censure shall degrade or depose any man from any
Civill dignitie, office, or Authoritie he shall have in the
Commonwealth."[11] An example of how strictly this rule
could be applied occurred three years later when the town
of Gloucester attempted to dismiss a representative to the
General Court who got in trouble with the church imme-
diately after his election. Before the Court sessions began,
the town elected another man and sent him to present his
credentials, but the Court sent the second representative
home and insisted that the town abide by its first choice.[12]

The distinction between ecclesiastical and civil authority
did not find expression in any law to exclude clergymen
from civil office, but public opinion on this matter is indicated by the fact that clergymen did not hold public office
in the government of early Massachusetts. In 1632, when
the settlers were feeling out the boundaries of the church,
the question arose in Boston whether a ruling elder might
at the same time be a civil magistrate. A ruling elder was
not regarded as a clergyman: he was a lay officer of the
church, like a deacon. Nevertheless, when the church of

Boston consulted the other churches of the colony about the question, they all agreed that not even this minor office in the church could be held by a man who was also an officer of the civil government.[13]

The settlers of Connecticut were less strict, to their detriment, Winthrop thought. They failed, he said, to choose men of learning and judgment as civil magistrates. And because these officers were not up to their job, "the main burden for managing of state business fell upon some one or other of their ministers . . . who, though they were men of singular wisdom and godliness, yet, stepping out of their course, their actions wanted that blessing, which otherwise might have been expected." [14]

In Massachusetts the civil government, staffed entirely by laymen, assumed control over the temporal matters that the ecclesiastical courts governed in England: probating of wills and all cases of marriage and divorce. Marriage was completely secularized—so much so that only civil officers were authorized to marry couples.[15] Ministers were sometimes present at a wedding and might offer a few words of spiritual advice, but the government was wary of this practice. Once when a marriage was about to be performed in Boston and it had been arranged that the Reverend Peter Hobart of Hingham should preach at it, Winthrop and his fellow magistrates forbade any sermon, lest it be a means of introducing ministerial weddings.[16]

Over religious and moral offenses the civil government exercised a jurisdiction concurrent with but broader than that of the individual churches; while the churches were responsible for disciplining only their own members, the state was responsible for the spiritual welfare of every man within its borders, whether church member or not. A church member accused of heresy or adultery or usury or any other sin would therefore be subject to both rebuke

by the church and punishment by the state, but each body
would operate independently of the other and with different
sanctions. The state sometimes made use of the same ad-
monitory procedure that the churches employed, but behind
the state's admonition was the threat not of excommunication, with which the state could have nothing to do, but of
fine, imprisonment, or exile. How eloquently such a threat
might speak in the laconic idiom of New England is
suggested by an item in the Massachusetts records for March
13, 1639: "Mr. Thomas Makepeace, because of his novile
disposition, was informed wee were weary of him unless
hee reforme." [17] A more powerful suggestion has never, perhaps, been conveyed with greater economy of language.

There was some difference of opinion among Puritans as
to whether the state ought to proceed against church members before the church had acted, especially in cases of
heresy. At the time of the trouble over Anne Hutchinson
in 1637, a number of ministers, when asked for their views
on the subject, stated that while the government might
punish manifest and dangerous heresies without waiting for
the church, the judgment of the church should be given
first in doubtful cases.[18] This opinion, though of course not
binding, seems to have expressed a feeling on the part of
some persons that the actions of church and state should
be co-ordinated in cases involving church members. In the
following year, 1638, the government actually did forbear
taking action against a minor vice in the hope that the
church might be able to deal with it. Winthrop recorded
in his diary that the General Court, concerned about the
multitude of costly new fashions in clothes, summoned the
ministers of the churches, "and laid it upon them, as belonging to them, to redress it, by urging it upon the consciences
of their people, which they promised to do." The results
were disappointing because, according to Winthrop, the

ministers' wives "were in some measure partners in this general disorder." [19] The next year the Court gave the ministers another chance, but warned them that henceforth all breaches of the sumptuary laws would be treated as contempt of authority (and would therefore be punished by the civil government).[20]

Perhaps as a result of this warning, some of the ministers presented the Court with a memorandum in which they maintained that the civil government should not proceed against a church member for any kind of offense, until the church had dealt with him. According to Winthrop, the Court would not accept this restraint, "and it appeared, indeed, that divers of the elders [ministers] [21] did not agree in those points." [22] The next year, 1641, the magistrates showed that their decision was final, when the constable of Boston, upon being required to jail a church member, questioned the authority of the magistrates to act until the church had dealt with the man. For this insolent behavior, Winthrop tells us, the constable himself was jailed and released only after confessing his error, with a fine of twenty shillings for his contempt of authority.[23]

Among the magistrates of early Massachusetts, Winthrop was probably the most insistent on this independence of the civil government from the control of the churches. It was his view that a civil magistrate must not be dealt with by his church for any action arising out of his magisterial office. The ministers themselves agreed early in 1637 that "no member of the court ought to be publicly questioned by a church for any speech in the court, without the license of the court." [24] This was a considerable concession to the civil power, for a civil magistrate, as a member of a particular church, was generally considered to be subject to the spiritual discipline of that church.[25] A few months after the ministers had given this opinion, the members of Winthrop's

church became incensed with him for some of his proceedings in the case of Anne Hutchinson and prepared to call
him to account. Winthrop forestalled them by explaining
why they could not properly discipline him for anything
he did in the civil government. "It is true, indeed," he admitted, "that magistrates, as they are church members, are
accountable to the church for their failings, but that is when
they are out of their calling. . . . If a magistrate shall, in
a private way, take away a man's goods or his servants, etc.,
the church may call him to account for it; but if he doth
thus in pursuing a course of justice, (though the thing be
unjust,) yet he is not accountable." [26]

With these arguments Winthrop was able to prevent the
church from taking action against him, and within a few
months the members were reconciled to what he had done.
But in 1641 the civil government formally renounced the
exemption Winthrop had claimed for it, by declaring that
every church had liberty to deal "in a church way" with
officers of government for their actions in office, provided
"it be done with due observance and respect." [27] This, of
course, did not mean that church discipline would have any
effect on the public authority of the magistrate in question.
Indeed this declaration was accompanied by the other one,
already noticed, to the effect that no church censure could
degrade or depose a man from civil office. Thus the independence of the churches and of the government were both
vindicated, but the superiority that Winthrop demanded
for the civil government was reduced.

Another problem which caused some initial disagreement
among orthodox New Englanders was the support of the
ministry. The salary of an English minister came from the
income of endowments or legacies belonging to the office in
his particular parish, from the income of lands belonging to
the church, and from tithes, the customary tax of one-tenth

laid upon the produce of the inhabitants of the parish.
In Massachusetts one of the first acts of Winthrop's government, in November, 1630, was to levy a tax for the support
of the two ministers then preaching in the colony.[28] After
this date, for the next seven years the various churches seem
to have provided for their ministers by voluntary contribution, and there were many who believed (with the Separatists) that this was the only proper procedure. The
difficulty was that some of the non-members felt no obligation to contribute, and in some towns the number of members was too small to bear the burden. The General Court
therefore, having ordered in 1635 that non-members must
attend church, decided in 1638 that they should help to pay
for the preaching that might lead ultimately to their conversion. Where voluntary contributions failed, the inhabitants of a town, whether church members or not, must
be taxed by the civil government to raise the necessary
amount.[29]

Voluntary contributions may have continued to be the
rule for some time in towns where conscientious ministers
feared that a fixed and certain income, collected by compulsion, would be a corrupting influence on men of their
profession. In 1639 Winthrop reported a sermon at Boston,
in which John Cotton warned his congregation "that when
magistrates are forced to provide for the maintenance of
ministers etc., then the churches are in a declining condition . . . that the ministers' maintenance should be by
voluntary contribution, not by lands, or revenues, or tithes,
etc.; for these have always been accompanied with pride, contention, and sloth." [30] In spite of Cotton's warning, the magistrates did have to levy taxes in many towns, but such
support given the church by the state was not, to the Puritan,
a violation of the distinction between the two jurisdictions.
Had the church attempted to enforce collection of dues by

itself, admonishing or excommunicating members for failure to pay, this would have been an unwarranted intrusion of the church into temporal matters. But the state in levying payments for the support of ministers, as in requiring everyone to hear their sermons, was operating in its proper sphere, protecting the spiritual welfare of all its subjects.

Where the rulers of Massachusetts came closest to confounding the boundary between church and state was in an act passed in 1631, confining the right of voting and holding public office to church members.[31] Roger Williams was not the only one to perceive the danger in this measure. Lord Saye and Sele, a Puritan nobleman interested in New England, feared that it would result in an attempt by the church to dominate the civil government. The leaders of Massachusetts could only reply that they had set up sufficient safeguards to prevent such a development. John Cotton wrote to his lordship that "magistrates are neyther chosen to office in the church, nor doe governe by directions from the church, but by civill lawes, and those enacted in generall corts, and executed in corts of justice, by the governors and assistants. In all which, the church (as the church) hath nothing to doe: only, it prepareth fitt instruments both to rule, and to choose rulers, which is no ambition in the church, nor dishonor to the commonwealth." [32]

The answer did not convince Lord Saye, and this was certainly the weak spot in the barrier which the Puritans erected against temporal activities by the church. Where all members of the government were members of a church and the whole society was dedicated to carrying out the will of God, the way was open for ambitious clergymen to meddle behind the scenes in secular affairs and achieve at least an informal and indirect control over the state. And there is a good deal of evidence of a tendency on the part of some clergymen to engage in this kind of political adventure.

For example, in the election of 1640, when Winthrop had occupied the governor's chair for three successive years (he had also occupied it from 1630 to 1634), the ministers took it upon themselves to persuade their congregations that it was dangerous to continue one man in the highest office for so long, lest he attain a kind of life tenure and perhaps even establish a hereditary governorship. The ministers came to Winthrop and explained that they were moved by no dislike of him or his government, and he gracefully withdrew in favor of Thomas Dudley. Thus the ministers, though without any political authority, were nevertheless able to affect a purely political matter.[33]

The civil government, moreover, seems to have welcomed the influence and advice of the clergy, so long as they did not seek to make it compulsory. Puritan ministers were learned men, full of scholarly information that might be of use to rulers who were trying to translate scriptural injunctions into workable policy. Each year at the time when a new General Court was chosen, the government appointed a minister to preach an "election sermon" which instructed the voters about the nature of government and the kind of men fit to rule. And frequently during the year the men whom the voters elected to office consulted the ministers about affairs of state: about relations with the Indians and relations with England, about codes of law and cases at law. That the ministers ought to play an advisory role in a Puritan state seems to have been regarded as obvious: once when Winthrop neglected to consult them before giving assistance to a French adventurer, he acknowledged his error.[34] On another occasion Thomas Dudley was rebuked for disrespect to Ezekiel Rogers, the peppery individual who ministered to the church at Rowley. Rogers had come to plead Rowley's case in a dispute; Dudley flared up at this ministerial intervention and cried out, "Do you think to come with your eldership here to carry matters?" Dudley could see nothing wrong with his statement, but the other magistrates persuaded him to apologize.[35]

The great respect that the magistrates paid the clergy was based on more than personal esteem and a genuinely felt need for advice. Because of the veneration in which the ministers were held by their congregations, they were able to exert a salutary influence among the people in support of the magistrates' authority. As Winthrop put it in a letter to the Earl of Warwick, "The Ministers have great power with the people, wherby throughe the good correspondency between the magistrates and them, they are the more easly governed." [36]

This particular usefulness of the clergy not only prompted the magistrates to be respectful themselves but also made them shy away from taking any action that might diminish the peoples' respect. Winthrop records an episode in 1639 when the government became concerned about the multiplication of lectures (sermons given on weekdays) in the various churches. The ministers were requested by an order of court to consider the great neglect of work that resulted from this multitude of lectures and to come to some agreement about limiting the number of them. To the ministers this seemed like an intrusion of the government into spiritual affairs, and there was much argument about whether the government had any right to make such a request. The magistrates were persuaded that it did, but they forbore to press the point lest they weaken the position of the ministers. Again, Winthrop explained: "The elders had great power in the people's hearts, which was needful to be upheld, lest the people should break their bonds through abuse of liberty, which divers, having surfeited of, were very forward to incite others to raise mutinies and foment dangerous and groundless jealousies of the magistrates, etc., which the wisdom and care of the elders did still prevail against; and indeed the people themselves, generally, through the churches, were of that understanding and moderation, as they would easily be guided in their way by any rule from scripture or sound reason." [37]

It would appear, then, that while the clergy could exercise no temporal power officially, the possibility of a very extensive influence was open to them. But one must beware of exaggerating this influence. The clergy of New England were not a corporate body. A minister was a minister only with respect to his own church, and if ministers occasionally met in synods to determine difficult questions of policy, the meetings were not regular and their determinations were not binding. On many questions clerical opinion varied widely. No man or group of men was entitled to speak for the church in Massachusetts. Indeed New Englanders knew no such thing as *the* church. Before Roger Williams founded Rhode Island, there was probably no place in the western world where clergymen were as carefully cut off from political power as in Massachusetts Bay.

The New Israel

It must nevertheless be apparent that the exclusion of the Massachusetts churches and clergy from civil power was not accompanied by a corresponding release of the state from religious responsibilities. Indeed the same fear of Rome that debarred the clergy from government placed the hand of the ruler directly in that of God and thus enhanced his authority as guardian of the church. Although the Puritans never went as far as King James in his apotheosis of the monarch, the very fact that they elected their rulers annually perhaps made them insist the more strenuously on the intimacy of

the governor with God, lest the brevity of his tenure of
office diminish respect for his authority. Puritan ministers,
like King James, cited the eighty-second psalm to show that
God himself addressed civil rulers as gods. And Winthrop
repeatedly reminded the voters who elected him that while
in office he drew his authority not from them, but directly
from God.

This claim of civil rulers to divine authority was not
peculiar to Puritans or to Englishmen. In the rise of national states in the sixteenth century, the kings who had
wrested powers from barons and princes often preferred to
accept commissions from God rather than Rome. But Englishmen and their kings seem to have claimed a more inti-
mate association with the Almighty than did other nations.
Behind the claims of a John Winthrop or an Oliver Cromwell to be the arm of God's will lay not only the years of
antipapal arguments but also that century of optimism in
which Englishmen had persuaded themselves that they,
above all other nations, had a divine mission in the world.
As we have seen, their confidence that England was an elect
nation, the successor of Israel, had been shaken by the drift
of the Stuart monarchy in the first decades of the seventeenth century. For a time it had seemed that God would
surely destroy a people who so little honored their obligation
to obey Him. Puritan preachers had issued warnings of the
judgments that He might inflict. If, cried Robert Gray in
1609, "God once visit this land and citie, for the sinnes of
the inhabitants thereof, neither this nor that, neither the
largeness of their territories, nor their beauty, excellence,
riches, or multitude of people shall excuse them, but he
will make them as Sodom, and like unto Gomorrha." [38] In
the succeeding years, as the Church of England hardened
in its half-reformed condition and James I gave place to
Charles I, who had even less use for Puritans than had his

father, the cries of alarm grew louder. With a sense of impending doom, the founders of New England had pulled out of England to escape the heavy affliction that they felt was coming and to find a refuge where the true faith might be preserved in case God should permit Antichrist to destroy it in England.[39]

In spite of their forebodings, however, the settlers carried with them to the New World a pride in being English. Even the Separatists at Plymouth accepted as fact the view that England was the birthplace of the Reformation, and they had left Holland in part out of a fear that their children would grow up into Dutchmen.[40] The New World offered a way of remaining English, with all that that meant, and yet of escaping the fury that God must surely loose against His backsliding favorites. Many of the settlers thought of the move as a strategic retreat to a position from which a saving remnant could return to the fight later.

Many did return when the calling of the Long Parliament signaled the downfall of the king's Antichristian counsellors.[41] But meanwhile a majority of settlers had transferred to New England, and particularly to Massachusetts, the sense of a special mission that had formerly attached to England. England's covenant with God had been jeopardized, if not forfeited, by the failure of her monarchs to press forward in the reforms so happily begun. Massachusetts, however, had taken up the cause and made its own covenant with God. In the eyes of its founders Massachusetts was at once a new Israel and a new England.

There was, to be sure, no formal covenanting ceremony in which the Lord pledged himself to the people of Massachusetts, but New England's Moses, John Winthrop, told the emigrants, before they even set foot in America, how God had entered into agreement with them. In a famous speech aboard the *Arbella* he explained that God "hath

taken us to be his after a most strickt and peculiar manner
. . . wee are entered into Covenant with him for this
worke, wee have taken out a Commission. . . . Now if the
Lord shall please to heare us, and bring us in peace to the
place wee desire, then hath hee ratified this Covenant and
sealed our Commission, [and] will expect a strickt per-
formance of the Articles contained in it. . . ." [42]

The belief that Winthrop here expressed made everything
that happened in early Massachusetts pregnant with meaning. All events must be sifted for clues to the colony's
success or failure in satisfying the terms of God's covenant.
The fact that He had devastated the Indians of the region
by a plague before the settlement began was taken as con-
firmation of the colony's special relationship with Him.
Peace, prosperity, and good harvests were tokens of His
approval and cause for days of formal, solemn thanksgiving.
On the other hand, drought, disease, and disaster of any
kind were the more terrible because they represented God's
disapproval. In response to them the government appointed
days of fasting, when everyone searched his soul and humbled himself for the sins that had prompted God's dis-
pleasure.

For the good of all future men, and especially Englishmen, it was urgent that the holy mission of Massachusetts
should succeed; Winthrop, with a full sense of the colony's
importance in the history of the world, recorded its daily
progress with close attention to the events by which God
signalized His favor. And Winthrop was by no means the
only one tracking the course of God's wonder-working providence in New England. Seldom has a people been so well
supplied with historians, and the lesson they drew was always the same: that God rewarded the obedience of His
chosen covenant people with prosperity and their disobedience with adversity. Adversity did not necessarily mean that

the covenant was lost. God was patient with His people and might remind them of their duties by a long succession of troubles before He gave them up as hopeless. But wrath was the ultimate reward when His Israel failed to profit by the strokes of His rod.[48]

Like others who have claimed the special attention of God, the New Englanders did not simply record His rewards and punishments but deliberately sought His favor. Everyone in the land was expected to exert himself to this purpose, but official responsibility for keeping the covenant lay with the state. Individuals might worry about their neighbors' behavior or their own; but in the end it was the business of civil government to enforce obedience to God and thus retain His favor for the colony.

The weight of this responsibility in determining the actions of the Massachusetts government would be hard to exaggerate. One of the most graphic illustrations followed the outbreak of King Philip's War in 1675. When faced with the danger of extermination, the government did not fail to look after its military defenses at once, but its next step was to search out the "provoking evils" that had prompted God to chastise the country. The General Court passed a series of laws against long hair, excess in apparel, disorderly children, idleness, oppression, tippling, and Quakers.[44] The laws were preceded by a preamble that pointed to the whole rationale of government among a covenanted people:

Whereas the most wise and holy God, for severall years past, hath not only warned us by his word, but chastized us with his rods, inflicting upon us many generall (though lesser) judgments, but we have neither heard the word nor rod as wee ought, so as to be effectually humbled for our sinns to repent of them, reforme, and amend our wayes; hence it is the righteous God hath heightened our calamity, and given commission to the barbarous heathen to rise up against us, and to become a smart rod and severe scourge to us, in burning and depopulating severall hopefull plantations, murdering many of our people of all sorts, and seeming as it were to cast us off, and putting us to shame, and not going forth with our armies, heereby speaking aloud to us to search and try our wayes, and turne againe unto the Lord our God, from whom wee have departed with a great backsliding.[45]

Among the terms of the covenant that government must enforce, foremost was the preservation and protection of true religion. Hence the act against Quakers that followed this preamble. Hence the persecution of other heretics. Hence too the government tax for support of the clergy. The Puritan principle of separation of church and state did not absolve the state from its covenant-imposed responsibility for the church. And the Puritan belief that officers of government were agents of God made it doubly imperative that they protect, nourish, and maintain *His* religion and *His* church to the exclusion of all rivals. The governors of Massachusetts and the men they ruled believed that every government in the world had the same duty to protect true religion and the true church, but it seemed that in the existing phase of the Christian struggle against Antichrist only Massachusetts recognized her responsibility.

The mantle of Israel, lost by England's Stuart kings, had descended on Massachusetts. The colony was not a theocracy in the usual sense of a rule by priests. But in the sense of a rule by God, through agents who steadily searched His Word and sought to apply it to every situation, Massachusetts aspired to be a theocracy. The actuality would inevitably fall short of the aspiration, because of human corruption; but men could take a pride and joy in trying, especially when they could feel that they led the whole world.

Only when we have acknowledged New England's achievement in separating church and state, and only when we
understand its sense of mission as the new Israel, can we
appreciate the dismay that Roger Williams caused his contemporaries. And only then can we appreciate his intellectual daring. For, as will be seen, Williams demanded the
separation of the state not merely from the church but from
God.

IV

The Basis of Government

THE CAST of Williams' mind, Perry Miller has reminded us, was theological, rather than social or political.[1] And theological it certainly was, if we take the statement to mean that Williams' every thought took its rise from religion. But in his writings, from which alone we can know his mind, Williams was more often concerned with ecclesiastical and political institutions than with theology. Except in two or three treatises, he was moved to write only when he found church or state engaged in activities he disapproved. Moreover, his own thinking seems to have been orthodox except where it touched institutions. He quarreled with the Puritans of Massachusetts not because he disliked their theology—he defended it against the Quakers'[2]—but because he disliked their institutions.

While he remained in Massachusetts, the imperfections of the church bothered him more than those of the state. For some time after he left the colony he went on with his efforts to purify the membership. Even after he persuaded himself that the church had expired and that human efforts could not revive it, he continued to study the institutional forms that Christ had appointed for it. He argued about them with John Cotton and with the Quakers, and he offered suggestions to the English Puritans who began remodeling the mother country's churches after 1641. But the expression of his ideas was necessarily inhibited by his unwillingness, at least in print, to persuade others to his own churchless way of life. No such difficulty impeded his writing and thinking about the state. However theological the cast of his mind, he wrote most often, most effectively, and most significantly about civil government.

A Covenant Without God

One starting point of Williams' thinking about politics was the widely accepted idea that government originates in an agreement between rulers and people. Although the idea was an old one, the Puritans of old England and New had readily assimilated it and found no difficulty in reconciling it with their belief that government is an ordinance of God, ordained and established by Him in order to hold in check the evil propensities of fallen man. Rulers, the Puritans said, were God's vicegerents, agents appointed to enforce His will, but His manner of appointing them was indirect: He gave authority initially to a whole people and allowed them to pass it on, through a covenant, to rulers.

The proceeding was much the same as that followed in the formation of a church: men agreed with one another and with God to be a people (or a church) and then in the name of God chose rulers (or ministers) to govern them. There were two distinct steps involved. A group of individuals or families became a people by making a covenant

with God in which they agreed to obey His laws. Having
thus become a people, they created a government in a
second covenant endowing rulers with authority to enforce
those laws. The two steps might be almost simultaneous,
and in their thinking about the state the Puritans commonly
blended the two covenants into one and made God the
author of it. Although the only visible activity in forming
the covenants was on the part of the people or their rulers,
God was thought to be a party to all the proceedings. It
was His power, not their own, that the people gave to
rulers.[3]

Williams agreed that political power came to government
from the people and that it was up to the people to measure
it out to their rulers in a covenant that bound both parties.
But he had his own ideas about the role of God in this
process. The God of Roger Williams was a real and un-
mistakable God, who did not enter into the transactions
of men in so light a manner as to be unperceived. If He
had given political power to a group of people, there would
be no mistaking the fact that He had done it. John
Winthrop might persuade himself that God had sealed a
covenant with Massachusetts simply by bringing a company
of people safely across the Atlantic Ocean. Roger Williams
could not. John Winthrop might see the hand of God offering him authority whenever the voters of Massachusetts cast
their ballots for him. Roger Williams could not. And when
Puritans talked of the divine right of kings or of the people's
holding the powers of government in trust for the Almighty,
Williams wanted to see the deed of gift. Where and when
and how, he wanted to know, did God transfer His powers
to the people or anyone else?

For that matter, when and where and how did God take
any people since the Jews into covenant with Him? If He
did so momentous a thing, He would scarcely leave the

people unaware of it. It would not require a speech by John Winthrop to make the fact known. To read the presence of God into human transactions was blasphemous. To claim a divine origin for any government was to be guilty of the same presumption that the Quakers showed in calling their "inner light" the voice of God and that Puritans showed in assuming that God stood behind churches He had never authorized and ministers He had never called. To Williams the Bible clearly revealed that God established His church and ministry through Christ and that Christ continued it through apostles and evangelists. There had to be a visible, temporal specific transfer of powers. An agreement of self-appointed saints could not make a church or a minister.

By contrast, an agreement of self-appointed subjects *could* make a government and *could* make rulers. What such an agreement could not do was to endow rulers with divine sanction or with powers that belonged to God. Williams acknowledged that God approved of government in the same way that He approved of marriage and disapproved of adultery.[4] Civil government was a good thing: Williams would not have wished to live without it. But it had no access to divinity. It originated in and gained its powers from the people; and the people could not convey to it any powers they did not themselves possess. Emphatically absent from any powers possessed by the people was the capacity to start churches; and if they could not start churches, they could scarcely claim a right to control them. Therefore they could not delegate such control to rulers.

In denying government authority over religion or churches, Williams marched in a direction that few Englishmen or Americans (not to speak of Europeans) would be ready to follow for a century or more. The early Separatists had edged toward freeing the church from state control when

they insisted that Christians must not await orders or per-
mission from civil rulers before reforming their churches.
"Reformation without tarrying for any" meant without
waiting for the civil government. But in spite of Robert
Brown's rousing slogan, the Separatists had actually believed
that the state *ought* to control religion, that the government
ought to require everybody who worshipped to worship
the way the Separatists did. It was only when the government failed in its custodial role that Christians must act
without it.[5] But for Williams the government had no business with the church at all.

Williams seems to have reached his conclusion in some
intuitive way before he had fully articulated the premises
that underlay it. As early as April, 1631, Winthrop reported
Williams' opinion that a magistrate might not punish a
breach of the first table (the first four commandments, which
concern religion).[6] But Williams was not ready to write on
the subject until he went to England in 1643. In explaining
and defending his political convictions in the tracts he
published there, Williams did not feel obliged to defend his
basic assumption that government originates in an agreement—a covenant—of the people, for this was an accepted
idea. But in evicting God from the proceedings he took a
step that was all but incomprehensible to his contemporaries
(and a little too easily comprehensible to his nineteenth-
and twentieth-century descendants).

At the root of his reasoning, another of the many starting
points that all led Williams to the same vision of a proper
state, lay a novel reading of history, which, like his other
intellectual novelties, rested on widely accepted assumptions.
From the time of the Church Fathers, Christian theologians
had made it their task to reconcile the events of the Old
Testament with those of the New. Out of their efforts developed a branch of theology known as typology, devoted

to discovering in the history of Israel certain persons, events, and episodes that somehow prefigured the life of Christ. For example, Joseph's descent into the pit and Jonah's into the belly of the whale prefigured Christ's descent into hell. Solomon's temple prefigured the church of Christ. In typological terms, Joseph and Jonah were "types" of Christ and Christ was the "antitype" of Joseph and Jonah; the temple was a type of the church and the church was the antitype of the temple. With the coming of Christ the events recorded in the Old Testament acquired or retained their significance as types, for the instruction of future generations of Christians, but some, at least, of the literal significance of many of those events departed. Christians were called upon to imitate not Joseph or Jonah but Christ. Christ thus wrought a break in the continuity of history that could be bridged only by deciphering the symbolism of the history that preceded Him.[7]

Not everything in the Old Testament was typological: the Ten Commandments, for example, were as literally significant and binding for Christians as they had been for Jews. But theologians disagreed about precisely which events or institutions were to be interpreted typologically and which were not. Probably most Protestant divines of the seventeenth century made some use of typology, but not to the point of assuming that the Old Testament could be read only or primarily typologically. For many, typology was no more than a way of giving additional, figurative meaning to events that also retained their literal significance. Williams, as was his wont, insisted on a more rigorous division. Instead of using typology as an instrument to reconcile the Old Testament with the New, he bent the instrument to differentiate the two more sharply. Although he admitted that some of the precepts of the Old Testament retained a universal validity, his usual demand was that the

Old Testament be read in a typological sense. In trying to read it literally, men too often forgot the gap between themselves and their Maker; though the age of revelation was past, they identified themselves with the holy men to whom God had spoken directly. The danger was great among rulers, who were easily tempted to see themselves as modern counterparts of the rulers of Israel. When a Christian prince or magistrate imitated a Joshua or a David, he tried to turn back the clock to a time forever lost.

It was futile and wrong for civil rulers to learn from Israel, because Israel could have no modern counterpart. Williams agreed with other Puritans and Protestants that Israel had been a nation specially favored by God and that in Israel God had combined state and church in a single holy institution. But Williams believed that with the coming of Christ, God had dissolved the combination, that to accomplish the dissolution was in fact one of His purposes in sending Christ into the world. In examining the consequences of the incarnation, Williams found that the Jewish church ceased to be the church of God; the Jews became an ordinary nation on a par with other nations; and the Israel of the Old Testament assumed a purely typological significance. The ecclesiastical function of Israel was passed on to spiritual associations, to groups of believers who gathered to worship God and His son, wholly unconnected with civil government. These early Christian churches and their successors were the antitype of Israel; and in the antitype the temporal powers of the old church-state of Israel were transformed into purely spiritual powers. The only sword Christ allowed His church was spiritual, the "two-edged sword" [8] coming out of His mouth; the church's only power was the power of the Word. Since Christian churches must not have temporal power and civil states must, a combined church-state composed of Christians was an impossibility and Israel as a church-state could have no literal significance for man in the Christian era. And typologically, Israel itself, and not merely its temple, was the Old Testament prefiguration of the New Testament church of Christ.[9]

The implications of Williams' typological interpretation were far-reaching, especially for civil government, because so many misguided magistrates had sought instruction where there was none to be had. The devotion of New Englanders to the example of Israel was the great obstacle that prevented them from discerning the true functions of government. To take Israel as a model for the state, the way the leaders of Massachusetts had done, was to haul down Christ and restore Moses. In the opening of *The Bloody Tenent yet more Bloody* Williams explained that the basis of all his reasoning lay in two propositions:

First that the People (the Original of all free Power and Government) are not invested with Power from Christ Jesus, to rule his Wife or Church, to keep it pure, to punish Opposites by force of Armes. etc.

Secondly, that the Pattern of the National Church of Israel, was a None-such, unimitable by any Civil State, in all or any of the Nations of the World beside.[10]

The two propositions were closely related. Israel was unique in the history of the world and unimitable, Williams believed, because while God had for a time placed both His government and His religion on earth in the safekeeping of the people of Israel, He had never again entered into covenant with any nation. No subsequent government had His sponsorship; none was authorized to act in His behalf. Since the coming of Christ the only way God had contracted with men, except as individuals, was through the churches of Christ, which were scattered throughout the nations and were forbidden by their founder to propagate or defend His religion by force. Moses could wield the sword for God with righteousness. Israel could send forth its armies to smite the heathen. But no body of men who now employed force in defense of religion, whether at home or abroad, could claim the name of Christian. Force could be successfully exercised in religion only in support of false, unchristian religions. Any religion that could benefit from the use of force was by definition not Christian.

It did not follow that Christians needed no governments. Governments there must be, and Christians must join other men in establishing them and submitting to them. But no government should expect the divine assistance, guidance, and authority that God had given Israel. Parliament might go through the motions of imposing a solemn league and covenant on England, as it did in 1643, but neither God nor Christ would be party to a covenant designed by men and enacted by men. Parliament could exercise the authority of the people, but it was futile to claim a higher sponsorship. A government could have only the powers of the people who created it, and no people was now invested with religious powers. To suppose that a government had either a right or a duty to enforce true religion was to assume "that every Common-weale hath radically and fundamentally in it a power of true discerning the true feare of God, which they transfer to their Magistrates and Officers." [11] And such an assumption was palpably absurd.

What shocked Williams most about the position he opposed was that it subjected Christ's holy church and religion to the whims of men. If, as his opponents contended, magistrates received from the people an authority to establish true religion, it inevitably followed

that a people, as a people, naturally considered (of what Nature or Nation soever in Europe, Asia, Africa or America)

have fundamentally and originally, as men, a power to gov-
erne the Church, to see her doe her duty, to correct her, to
redresse, reforme, establish, etc. And if this be not to pull
God and Christ, and Spirit out of Heaven, and subject them
unto naturall, sinfull, inconstant men, and so consequently
to Sathan himselfe, by whom all peoples naturally are
guided, let Heaven and Earth judge.[12]

John Cotton attempted to answer this reasoning by confining the right to regulate religion to those magistrates who
were truly godly. And these, he suggested, should maintain
only the fundamental truths, not subsidiary details in which
there might be legitimate variations of opinion.[13] Such
distinctions Williams treated with scorn. If the establishment of true religion was any part of the magistrate's business, it must be an extremely important part, yet Cotton
was suggesting that a magistrate who happened to be unqualified in this matter should restrain himself from acting
in it: "It seemes indeed a marvelous, and yet it is Master
Cottons, conclusion, that such Magistrates, yea all or most
of the Magistrates that ever have been since Christ, and
now extant upon the face of the earth, must sit down, stay
and suspend, and that all their life long, from the executing
of the maine and principal part of their office, to wit, in
matters concerning the conscience, religion, and worship,
of the people." [14]

To put the problem in another way: if it was the duty
of a magistrate to protect religion, then he must either
leave his most solemn duty unfulfilled, or else he must do
it according to his best judgment. If his best judgment made
him a Mohammedan, a Jew, or a Roman Catholic, then he
must suppress all other religions, including that of Christ.
And in point of fact, since most men did accept the view
that Williams opposed, most magistrates, even those who

professed to be Christians, had suppressed the servants of
Christ in all ages. If Cotton's doctrine was that of Christ, if
Christ wished His church protected by the government, how
did it happen that He had not taken pains to furnish the
world with even nominally Christian magistrates for the
first three centuries of His church's existence? And how did
it happen thereafter that He forgot himself for a thousand
years together by "providing no other heads, but bloody
and Popish kings and Emperors"? [15]

The answer for Williams was simple: Christ did not
choose to uphold His church by temporal means. Christ's
kingdom, though in the world, must not be of the world.
His church and religion suffered when the kingdoms of this
world tried to protect them. In its first three centuries the
church flourished in the midst of persecution; but when
Constantine adopted it and undertook to stamp out other
beliefs, "then began the great Mysterie of the Churches
sleepe, the Gardens of Christs Churches turned into the
Wildernesse of Nationall Religion, and the World (under
Constantines Dominion) to the most unchristian Christendome." [16] The nationalization of religion had meant the
end of Christianity; and while churches remained national,
they could never be Christian.

The Puritans in old England and New had gone some
distance toward removing the state from the influence of
the church, but they had left the church at the mercy of the
state, had in fact endowed the state with religious responsibilities that it could fulfill only at the expense of true
Christianity. While the Long Parliament ruled England,
the king was no longer head of the nation's supposed church,
but dropping of a title made no difference, said Williams, if
the civil government still undertook to protect and establish
one religion, of which it must ultimately be the judge: "I
know that Civill Magistrates (in some places) have declined

the name of Head of the Church, and Ecclesiasticall Judge, yet can they not with good conscience decline the name, if they doe the worke." [17] And in England in the 1640's, Parliament was certainly doing the work, providing for the establishment of presbyteries, for the licensing of preachers, and for the collection of revenues to be paid to clergymen, who in turn meddled in the government.

In New England the situation might look a little better. The New Englanders denied that they had or wanted a national church. Their churches, they said, were entirely voluntary in origin, composed only of visible saints gathered from the world. And Williams could agree that the New Englanders came closer to Christ than old England had done. But the state still assumed responsibility for religion, supervised the formation of churches (and denied the right to any group it found unqualified or unorthodox), compelled non-members to attend the services, collected taxes for ministers' salaries, extended political rights only to church members, and summoned ministers to synods to determine ecclesiastical practices. In Williams' opinion these actions violated the Puritans' distinction of the differing spheres and methods of church and state, and made the churches of New England, like those of England, in effect a national church. "I affirm," he declared, "(what ever are the pretences, pleas and coverings to the contrary) that that Church estate, that religion and worship which is commanded or permitted to be but one in a country, nation or province (as was the Jews religion in that typical land of Canaan) that Church is not in the nature of the particular Churches of Christ, but in the nature of a Nationall or state Church." [18] The ultimate proof was the treatment of Williams himself. "Why," he asked Cotton, "was I not yet permitted to live in the world, or Common-weale [of Massachusetts], except for this reason, that the Common weale and Church is yet but one, and hee that is banished from the one, must necessarily bee banished from the other also." [19]

New Englanders justified their banishment of him and other heretics as protection of Christ's church; but Williams was sure that if the New England churches had been truly Christ's, they would have neither needed nor wanted this kind of protection. Christ protected His churches by the two-edged sword of the Spirit, exercised in preaching, discipline, and the sacraments. By accepting the alleged help of the temporal sword, a church proclaimed itself false. Williams thought the New England churches, except in their false non-apostolic origin, had once reached close to the true pattern. But the state by its protective actions had transformed them, implicitly at least, into a national church and New England into a new and spurious Canaan.[20]

It is not surprising that Williams' diagnosis of the condition of the church and its relation to the state proved unacceptable in both old England and New. Most men in the seventeenth century lacked Williams' confidence that God's true religion could take care of itself and that no one should lift a finger to defend it except by spiritual weapons. John Cotton could fairly pose a problem for which Williams had no answer likely to satisfy his contemporaries: "If Civill weapons be debarred from defending Religion, upon pretence, that Church-weapons are sufficient, and then no Churches nor Church-weapons to be found upon the face of the earth, then let all Seducers to Apostacy, Idolaters, and Hereticks, let them all rejoyce in an open doore of liberty and safety. . . ." [21] But Williams was not troubled. Heretics and idolaters had abounded too in the first three centuries after Christ, yet the church had grown. The Lord would care for His own in due time by the two-edged sword of the Word.

In the pages of his tracts, as he argued out his views, Williams did not wait for his opponents to point out the implications of his position or the conclusions to be drawn from his premises. In hasty, helter-skelter fashion he poured them out, excited by the way they fell into place. Arguments arising from various starting points all converged with a consistency that must derive from Truth, the character in whose mouth he often placed them. The torrent of words may sometimes have left his readers bewildered, and it surely left most of them unconvinced, but behind it lay the rare simplicity of an original mind. As Williams uncovered the various consequences of his ideas, he put human society in new perspective; and he demolished, for anyone who accepted his premises, some of the assumptions that encumbered the statesmen of his day and still haunt our own.

The Elect Nation

One of the obvious casualties of Williams' onslaught was the conception of Englishmen that they constituted an elect nation, in covenant with God like Israel of old. It went without saying that if Israel was only a type of the Christian church, then no modern state could claim to be its antitype or successor. But Williams did not rest his demonstration on typology alone. He turned to recent history.

Those who described England as a new Israel liked to extoll her kings and queens for defending the land against Antichrist. In answer, Williams reminded Englishmen of the religious somersaults they had turned at the direction of those monarchs. "Who knowes not," he asked, "how easie it is to turne, and turne, and turne againe whole Nations from one Religion to another? Who knowes not that within the compasse of one poore span of 12 yeares revolution, all

England hath become from halfe Papist, halfe Protestant, to be absolute Protestants; from absolute Protestants, to absolute Papists; from absolute Papists (changing as fashions) to absolute Protestants?" [22] Williams was referring to the changes that occurred from the end of the reign of Henry VIII to the accession of Elizabeth, and he was sure that the country could be whirled about as rapidly in his own time. England was a religious weathercock.

When Williams wrote, the Long Parliament had resumed the progress of reformation, halted since the time of Elizabeth; but this was no encouragement to him. The Parliament was as ready to enforce religion by the sword and the people as ready to submit to it as ever their fathers had been. "The renowned Parliament of England," Williams wrote in 1652, "hath justly deserved a crown of honour to all posterity, for breaking the teeth of the oppressing Bishops and their courts; but to wring the sword out of the hands of a few prelates, and to suffer it (willingly) to be wrung out of their own hands, by many thousand Presbyterians, or Independants, what is it but to change one wolfe or lyon for another, or in stead of one, to let loose the Dens of thousands?" [23] The sword that had turned England one way today would turn it another tomorrow. Before Christ should come again, Williams thought, it was not at all unlikely that England would be forced once more to do homage to the beast of Rome.[24]

All England's twistings and turnings would avail nothing, Williams believed, because Christ did not rule by the sword. This was perhaps the most obvious lesson of history, demonstrated generation after generation by unheeding zealots who presumed to act in God's name—and acted in vain. The self-imposed covenants of England or Massachusetts or any other people could confer no license to act in God's name or on His behalf. The authority of God in the existing phase

of history could be exercised by men only through the Word
in the mouth of a true believer. Every other claim to divine
authority, whether by Parliament or king, emperor or pope,
was imposture. "We read," Williams wrote in 1652,

of two mighty Princes professing the name of Christ, meet-
ing together in England; Charles the Fifth Emperour of
Germany, and Henry the Eighth of England: Their names
then soar'd so high for Christianity, that they were both in
Letters of Gold, set upon the very Gates of Guildhal in Lon-
don, Carolus Defensor Ecclesiae, Henricus Fidei: yet when
Luther, or the poorest follower of the truth of Christ Jesus
witnessed by Luther, were condemned and persecuted by
that Charles the Fifth, the great defender of the Church; I
ask, Who had the greatest Authority in Christs affaires, the
great Emperour Charles, or the poorest true Christian? And
when that glorious (pretended Defendour of the Faith)
Henry the Eighth, with all his Nobles and Bishops, sat in
person with so much Glory and Majesty, Terrour and Au-
thority, in that famous Disputation, and Condemnation of
that faithful witness of Christ Jesus John Lambert; I ask,
where was in truth the true Authority and power of Christ
Jesus, Whether in the stately assembly of Kings, Nobles, and
Bishops, or in the two-edged Sword of the Word and Spirit
of God, in the mouth of that one single, and yet most faith-
ful witness of Christ Jesus? [25]

For England to be an elect nation it would have to be
composed entirely of John Lamberts—that is, of true Christians—and this was precisely what could not happen to any
nation. The sword of state could make a whole nation of
hypocrites, but only God could make Christians, and God's
grace simply did not operate on a national scale. Anyone
who believed that Englishmen were Christians because they
were baptized was deceiving himself. "Christenings make

not Christians," Williams proclaimed, in his pamphlet of that name, and went on to demonstrate the impossibility of converting any nation as a whole, whether Indian or European.[26]

If England did not qualify as an elect nation, neither of course did New England. Some of the first emigrants may have told themselves that none but visible saints would come to Massachusetts; but most knew better, and three months at sea was enough to bring out the unregenerate character of the majority even before the holy experiment was launched. Winthrop, in explaining to his shipmates the special commission of Massachusetts, did not intend to suggest that God would place every member of the community among the elect in heaven. What he believed, and what several generations of New England ministers preached, was simply that God would bless the whole community in this world if it sought earnestly to fulfill its supposed covenant by establishing and enforcing His laws.

Williams not only denied that Massachusetts and the rest of New England had any special commission to enforce the laws of God; he also denied that those laws which had been given to Moses should be now enforced with the same rigor that the Israelites had practiced. It had been one of the grievances of English Puritans that the courts exacted only the lightest penalties for adultery while punishing many lesser crimes with death. In New England capital punishment was applied only to those crimes where the Bible specified it, thus reducing the total greatly from that in England, but the Bible did call for death to adulterers, and New England laws, outside Rhode Island, so provided. Williams never listed precisely what crimes he thought were worthy of death. The nearest he came to it was in a statement implying that "Adultery, Witchcraft etc." were not.[27] But he had no doubt that the slavish imitation of Israel in legal matters was as wrong as the government's attempt to regulate religion.[28]

To Williams the holy covenant that Winthrop claimed for Massachusetts was an unholy delusion. Winthrop and his fellow magistrates, in trying to reproduce the land of Canaan in New England, were ignoring the whole significance of Christ's incarnation. Since the birth of Christ, God favored no people with a covenant, and so it was wrong for any state "to set up a civill and temporall Israel, to bound out new Earthly holy Lands of Canaan" by exercising authority over religion in God's name.[29] There was nothing special in God's mind about England or New England or any other people or place in the world.

The Wrath of God

In releasing government from its supposed obligation to uphold true religion, Williams had to confront a lesson which thousands of Christians thought they had learned from history: when a people displeased God by failing to punish breaches of His commandments, especially those which concerned religion, then beware His wrath. History showed how Sodom and Gomorrha had suffered, not to mention Rome and countless other mighty cities and states that neglected His Word. God stood watch over the world and punished those peoples who allowed idolatry and vice to flourish amongst them. And His wrath was greatest against those who had lived foremost in His favor, against people with whom He had made a covenant that they failed to keep, against a backsliding Israel or England or Massachusetts. Fear of His wrath spurred the flight from old England to New and generated new impulses to reform whenever disaster or misfortune befell Massachusetts. When idolatry, heresy, or any other form of wickedness appeared, ministers would mount their pulpits to warn of God's wrath to come, and magistrates would busy themselves to restore or preserve divine favor by a more rigorous execution of God's laws. Fear of God equalled love of God among the Puritans. Fear guided—or misguided—their anachronistic imitation of Israel and blinded them, as Williams saw it, to the true facts of human history.

Williams, of course, acknowledged that Israel had come upon hard times when the government failed to uphold righteousness, and he also acknowledged that God might show His wrath against a true church—Israel's successor— that slipped from the faith once delivered to the saints. But his answer to the notion that God punished the nations of this world for permitting false worship was to look at the record. Was it in fact true that God punished a whole people for permitting idolatry? Like so many of the lessons that history is alleged to teach, this one, upon examination, turned out to be taught not very clearly, if at all.

As he read the record, it seemed to Williams to be true that "sooner or later the God of heaven punisheth the nations of the world, for their Idolatries, Superstitions, etc.," [30] but the time involved was more often later than sooner, and sometimes late enough to cast doubt on the directness of the relationship. Rome went for hundreds of years unpunished, Athens for thousands. Therefore, although "it pleaseth God sometimes to bring a people to utter destruction for their idolatry against himself, and cruelty against his people; yet we see the Lord doth not presently and instantly do this, but after a long course of many ages and generations, as was seen in Nineve her self, and since in Athens, Constantinople, and Rome both Pagan and Antichristian." [31]

Moreover, it was questionable whether peoples who did

suffer the wrath of God were punished for idolatry and false worship. The only, historians privy to God's motives were those who wrote the Bible; and in studying the historical causes they assigned for the destruction of Sodom, Williams found that there had been other provocations than idolatry, including oppression of the poor. In fact, more often than not, where the wrath of God did fall on a people it was for sins other than idolatry or false worship. Egypt, "though most infamous for Idolatry," did not suffer until its government oppressed the Jews. Israel, when guilty of idolatry, was not punished until it "mocked, and dispised, and mis-used the Messengers from God, sent unto them." Jerusalem was destroyed because it killed the prophets of Christ. And Revelation, that history of the future, foretold, in Chapter Eighteen, the destruction of Rome not for idolatry, but for her "Bloody Oppressions, to wit (verse the last) the blood of the Prophets and Saints, and of all that were slain upon the earth." In a word, the records showed that divine punishment was meted out to peoples not for tolerating false worship, but for persecuting the servants of God.[32]

In identifying this source of divine wrath, Williams was deliberately turning the tables on those who argued for religious intolerance as a means of escaping wrath. Throughout history the civil magistrates who exerted their powers to punish false prophets had succeeded only in offending God, for magistrates were generally incapable of recognizing a true servant of God when they saw one. Those who banished Roger Williams from Massachusetts, for example, had perhaps incurred in the eyes of God the very guilt they ostensibly sought to avoid. Although the concept of national guilt and punishment seemed to Williams a dubious doctrine, he did not hesitate thus to take advantage of his opponents' commitment to it.[33] But he gave far greater emphasis to the evil consequence that must follow from accepting the doctrine at all: right must ever be at the mercy of might, as had been so often demonstrated in the metamorphoses of English religion. If rulers were obliged to avert the wrath of God by stamping out heresy and idolatry, then "if one Magistrate, King or Parliament call this or that heresie, apostacie, etc. and make men say so will not a stronger Magistrate, King, Parliament, Army (that is, a stronger arm, or longer and more prosperous sword) call that heresie and Apostacie Truth and Christianity, and make men call it so?" [34] When Christians made the rulers of this world the guardians of their faith, the only result could be persecution of the true servants of Christ.

And besides, what was the idolatry that orthodox Puritans were so eager to stamp out? Was idolatry merely falling on one's knees before the cross or making graven images or chanting memorized prayers? If so, it might have been safe enough to assign to kings and judges and armies the responsibility for liberating the world from idolatry. But every Puritan knew that the roots of idolatry ran deep in every human heart, hidden from the hand that held the sword. Idolatry was honoring the creature more than the Creator. Idolatry was making too much of food and drink, raiment and riches. Idolatry was loving a wife or a child more than Christ. And here lay the supreme irony of the Puritans' attempt to stamp out idolatry in religion, for in New England as in old, Christians continued to make idols of the creatures. "The truth is," said Williams, "the great Gods of this world are God-belly, God-peace, God-wealth, God-honour, God-pleasure etc." [35] New Englanders, like every other people, worshipped these idols and even added another, "God Land," which Williams feared would become "as great a God with us English as God Gold was with the Spaniards." [36] What could be more ridiculous than the spectacle of a people pretending to put down idolatry, "When the whole World, and each Nation, and our Selves, lie in the second kind of Idolatry, of many sorts; Worshipping (according to the several Lusts of the Eye, the Flesh, and the Pride of Life) several sorts of Creatures, before the Creator." [37]

If God punished peoples for idolatry, then every people would be punished, for all were guilty and not least the people of New England. But God was not about to punish any people; in these days of Antichrist God did not concern Himself with whole peoples or nations or countries as such and would not do so until Christ's second coming. To read His favor or disfavor, His pleasure or wrath in the varying fortunes of any institution or people was self-deception, another piece of human presumption.

The Meaning of Adversity

It would be wrong to suppose that there was no subtlety in Puritan thought about the operation of God in human affairs. To be sure, it is easy to catch the first New Englanders exulting in the plagues and shipwrecks with which God struck down their enemies and in His remarkable deliverances of saints from peril. But the Puritans did not regard every happy event as a sign of God's special favor and every unhappy one as a sign of His anger. God might chastize His people like a watchful father, in order to correct them. He might try them with afflictions in order to wean them from too great love of the creature. Thus trouble might be a sign of God's loving help rather than of His wrath. Prosperity, on the other hand, might be none of God's doing but a temptation of Satan designed to plunge the unwary into that most perilous frame of mind, security. Few Puritans dared look upon success with complacency, and all Puritans were at their best in "improving" afflictions.

Nevertheless, in assessing the meaning of events, the orthodox Puritan generally made prosperity a reason for thanksgiving and affliction a reason for humiliation and rededication that would lead to better times. Although he was careful not to equate success with salvation, he generally welcomed it as something better than mere luck. And though he read every affliction as a spur to flagging moral efforts, he looked for God to crown his renewed efforts with some sign of approval. Such efforts could have nothing to do with eternal life, but in the Puritan's eye they had a great deal to do with the rewards and punishments that God allotted in this world, and especially to His covenanted people. Prosperity might be a temptation as well as a reward for good conduct, a source of uneasiness as well as a cause for thanksgiving, but it was the outcome that Puritans expected in their collective efforts to please God.[38]

When Roger Williams wrote his little treatise on Christian assurance, *Experiments of Spiritual Life and Health*, he posed in the preface a question about prosperity and adversity that he did not attempt to answer: "why is the Heart of a David himself (Psa. 30.) more apt to decline from God, upon the Mountaine of Joy, Deliverance, Victory, Prosperity, then in the dark Vale of the shadow of Death, Persecution, Sicknesse, Adversity"?[39] To the orthodox Puritan reader the question would have seemed appropriate. It pointed to one of those paradoxes of faith that remained inexplicable; but most Puritans, while allowing that prosperity could breed deadly security and idolatry of the creatures, did not go on from there to challenge the desirability of prosperity. Williams did, and therein lay the source of his deepest estrangement from other Puritans and from the whole subsequent American tradition that stems from Puritanism.

Williams, at some moments, was willing to allow that God might occasionally intervene in human affairs "to imprint a Character and Crown of his favour and love upon some Persons and Actions," and he cited as examples the defeat of the Spanish Armada, the success of the Parliamentary armies in the English civil wars, and the prosperity of the Netherlands.[40] But he thought such instances rare, too rare certainly to allow any man or group of men to measure the godliness of their conduct by the beneficial results it brought. If any general correlation existed, it was an inverse one: Mohammedans, papists, and other idolatrous and wicked men prospered, the Spaniards with their New World gold, the Turks with their endless conquests, while truly godly men were persecuted, "and the more Godly, the more persecuted." [41] It was equally true that "The neerer Christs followers have approached to worldly wealth, ease, liberty, honour, pleasure etc. . . . the further and further have they departed from God, from his Truth, from the Simplicitie, Power and Puritie of Christ Jesus and true Christianitie." [42]

At the opening of Williams' controversy with John Cotton, Cotton rebuked him with the fact that during his dispute with the ministers of Massachusetts before his banishment, he had been suddenly stricken with a heavy illness. This, Cotton suggested, should have humbled him to see the error of his ways. Instead, it had only quickened him to find errors in others. That Williams had not made the proper improvement of his affliction demonstrated his stubbornness to be the work of Satan.[43] It was a typical Puritan reading of an opponent's misfortune, and Williams' answer was a typical Williams answer. He acknowledged the need for soul searching to improve afflictions ("and what gracious fruit I reaped from that sicknes, I hope my soule shall never forget"), but he accepted affliction as the regular, predictable fate of Christ's servants in this world in the time of Antichrist: "and I have said and must say, and all Gods witnesses that have borne any paine or losse for Jesus, must say, that fellowship with the Lord Jesus in his sufferings is sweeter then all the fellowship with sinners, in all the profits, honours, and pleasures of this present evill world." [44]

Material success, as Williams saw it, was the award of the world, not of God; and the world, being sinful, bestowed its honors and prizes on sinners. The godly in this world were more apt to wear a crown of thorns and were not often to be found among the rich, the wellborn, and the honored. Christ was born of a poor carpenter's wife in a stable, and though He might have chosen hosts of angels to attend Him, instead he chose "Peter the Fisherman, and Paul the Tent-Maker." And so it had been ever since: among the servants of Christ were to be found "Not many Wise, not many Noble, not many Mighty." [45]

Williams here laid hold of an old idea. Many medieval depictions of hell contain a generous number of damned souls whose heads wear royal crown or bishop's mitre. But there was still a cutting edge to the idea when employed by a man who thought that prosperity bore an inverse ratio to godliness. His easiest victims were the clergy, or, rather, those who claimed that archaic title in an age when no true minister existed. Even if their callings could have been validated, Williams believed, they betrayed the falsity of their profession by denying the true, humble Christ. In every age since the coming of Antichrist, they had "disdain'd to serve a poore despised Christ, a Carpenter, one that came at last to the Gallowes, etc. And therefore have they ever framed to Themselves rich and Lordly, pompous and Princely, temporall and Wordly Christs, instead of the true Lord Jesus Christ." [46]

Williams was not thinking merely of the lordly prelates who had hounded the Puritans out of England. He had in mind his former colleagues in the ordinary ministry, both those who had settled in New England and those who had rid themselves of the prelacy in England. In England after the overthrow of Charles, the Puritan divines had "first made sure of an Ordinance of Parliament for Tithes and Maintenance, before any Ordinance for God himself." [47] And in New England the civil government taxed the inhabitants, regardless of whether they were church members or not, to support the ministry. Cotton could rightly answer that his own church at Boston supported him by voluntary contributions alone. "One swallow makes not a summer," replied Williams.[48]

In his opinion no servant of Christ, neither a so-called minister nor a layman who served Him as a witness or prophet, ought to accept a settled wage or maintenance for his service. A hireling ministry was none of Christ's, now or ever. Ministers might accept "the free and willing contribution of the Saints" (and Williams thought it the duty of saints to contribute if they could), but in its absence they must rely on "the diligent worke and labour of their owne hands." [49] Where Luther and Calvin had rejected the monastic life of prayer as no proper calling, Williams went a step further and denied that the ministry itself had ever been or ever could be a proper way to make a living: "He that makes a Trade of Preaching, that makes the cure of Souls, and the charge of mens eternall wellfare, a trade, a maintenance, and living, and that explicitely makes a covenant or bargain (and therefore no longer penny no longer Paternoster, no long[er] pay no longer pray, no longer Preach, no longer fast etc.) I am humbly confident to maintaine, that the Son of God never sent such a one to be a Labourer in his Vineyard." Neither the apostolical nor the feeding ministers described in the Scriptures were supported by "Wages, Tithes, Stipends, Sallaries." Instead they took what was given them, worked with their own hands night and day, supplying their own and others' wants. "And this was and will be the onely way of the Labourers of the Son of God." [50]

The lure of honor and gain that a state could dangle before the ministers it supported would ever cause their religious opinions to "tack about (as the Wind, and Time, and Advantage blows)." [51] And the same lure would attract men to a preaching career who had not been stirred by the spirit of God. Williams lashed out at the universities as the spawning ground of such uncalled preachers: "everyone that hath Friends may be preferred to Fellowships in Colledges, to the superstitious Degrees and Titles of Divinity (as they call it) and by these staires ascend up the Gospel preferments of rich and honourable Benefices." [52] Human learning he valued for its own sake (and was himself extraordinarily learned), but he scorned the "Monkish and idle course of life" led by students at universities, where marriage was forbidden and "to wet a finger in any pains or labor, it is a disgraceful and an unworthy Act." [53] It was desirable for a minister to know the ancient tongues in order to be able to read the Word of God in the original Hebrew and Greek, but there were other ways, he thought, of coming to this knowledge. The physically idle and financially cushioned life of a university scholar was the wrong apprenticeship for those who wished to follow in the difficult steps of Peter and Paul.[54]

In Williams' opinion a life of poverty and labor was the only appropriate one not merely for the clergy but for all true Christians. The Puritans' misreading of the Bible and their identification of themselves as the successors of Israel led them to misinterpret the meaning of prosperity and adversity in their own times. Because God had prospered

THE BASIS OF GOVERNMENT 113

Israel, they looked on worldly success as a sign of His favor to New England and on adversity as a sign of His disfavor. But adversity could hardly be a sign of God's disfavor when it was the commonest condition of His saints in this world. As for prosperity, said Williams, arguing again from typology, "such a temporall prosperity [as the Israelites enjoyed] of outward peace and plenty of all things, of increase of children, of cattell, of honour, of health, of successe, of victory, suits not temporally with the afflicted and persecuted estate of Gods people now: And therefore spirituall and soule blessednesse must be the Antitype, viz. in the midst of revilings, and all manner of evill speeches for christs sake, soul blessednesse. In the midst of afflictions and persecutions, soule blessednesse." [55] The only sign of God's favor in the present age, then, was spiritual prosperity, the gift of grace, which came only to individuals, never to a people.

In effect, Williams had reversed the accepted Puritan mode of understanding events. Adversity was not a sign of God's disfavor and prosperity was not ordinarily His way of rewarding men. In fact, true Christians should prefer adversity with its fellowship of godly men and shun prosperity, which was most often attained by ambitious, covetous, ruthless, and wicked men. Worldly success was most likely to be a sign of iniquity and of a need for serious soul searching. Said Williams: "outward peace, prosperity, riches, honor, is the portion of this world, notwithstanding their idolatries, apostacies, blasphemies: But the portion of Christs followers . . . paine and sorrow, yea poverty and persecution, untill the great day of refreshing, neer approaching." [56] The distance of Williams' departure from orthodoxy can be judged by comparing this passage with Increase Mather's exhortation to the government of Massachusetts after King Philip's War: "I know you cannot change mens hearts, yet you may doe much (if God help you) towards the effecting an outward Reformation, which will procure outward blessings and prevent outward Judgments and desolations." [57]

The orthodox position furnished a powerful motive for holding society as closely as possible within the laws of God, an incentive for good behavior more immediate than fear of hell or hope of heaven. If men behaved, they prospered; if not, they suffered. This proposition was not new when the Puritans espoused it, but they gave it a rationale, in the idea of a national covenant, that greatly increased its force. In later centuries, when the rationale lost its appeal through the decline of religious feeling, the idea retained an extraordinary momentum. It added an ingredient of self-righteousness to every enterprise that Americans undertook as a people. Whether they were overthrowing George III or sweeping across a continent or making the world safe for democracy, they enjoyed a sense of mission that made every success a sign of divine favor and every setback a spur to self-improvement.

From this tradition Roger Williams dissociated himself at its very beginning. If he had a successor among later Americans, it was Henry Thoreau, who lacked ambition, scorned success, and laughed at people who tried to reform the world, all because he was engaged in more important business than the world had to offer. But Thoreau was an anarchist. Williams was not. Though his aim was to abstract himself as far as possible from the dunghill of this world, he had a good many ideas about the way to run it. And by a curious irony, the idea on which he insisted most strongly, liberty of conscience, was rejected by his contemporaries, only to be adopted by a whole country which he would have found more apostate, more idolatrous, and more prosperous than his own New England.

V

The Business of Government

POLITICAL THINKERS have always concerned themselves with the state both as it is and as it ought to be. Roger Williams was no exception, but he shared with Machiavelli before him and with James Harrington in his own time a more than ordinary preoccupation with what *is*. The question was not really whether the church of Christ ought to be separated from the state: by its very nature the church *was* separate and ceased to be a church when it accepted state support. Similarly it was not a question whether a state could exist and exercise authority without supporting God's true religion: the fact was that states did exist, did exercise authority, and did prosper where the name of Christ was unknown.

The Art of Governing

Government, as Williams saw it, required skills that had nothing to do with religion. Other Puritans had already recognized that rulers sometimes had to do things which would be wrong in a private man. For example, it might in some cases be good "policy" for a ruler to practice deception, as Machiavelli had counselled. It might be right for a ruler to disobey God's laws in some exceptional instance, if by doing so he could make them prevail the better among his people. By such casuistry, Puritans managed to assimilate some of Machiavelli's doctrines even while denouncing him.[1] Williams, in repudiating the religious purposes of the state, threw over the Puritan effort to sanctify policy and recognized government more in Machiavelli's own terms as an art, like that of a pilot or of a soldier, an art with its own methods and purposes, useful to mankind, approved by God in a general way but human in origin and operation.

Christianity was not at odds with government. Indeed, Christ himself had given instructions to His followers that must make them good subjects of any government. Nor was it inconceivable that a Christian might participate in governing. Williams did not hold with those who thought that Christ had forbidden this. But he believed that, in point of fact, very few true Christians, either in the persecuted phase of Christianity before Constantine or in the apostate phase afterwards, had ever become magistrates. Christ had apparently known it would be so, for while He gave advice to His followers about their duties as subjects, He gave none about the way that Christians should conduct themselves as magistrates. Government in all ages had generally been left to men of high birth, great in wealth and wisdom, men of proven talent in the affairs of the world, and Williams never questioned the fitness of the coincidence. But since the world thus honored its own kind, and since Christ did not ordinarily honor those whom the world did, "since not many Wise and Noble are called, but the poore receive the Gospel, as God hath chosen the poore of the World to be rich in Faith," it was not to be expected that many Christians would be found among the rulers of the world.[2]

For the same reason it was foolish to look for rulers among Christians, to require as Massachusetts did that magistrates be chosen from church members. This was to deny the state access to political talent. The Massachusetts law would thrust into government persons unfit for it and at the same time waste the abilities of others who were fit: "we know the many excellent gifts wherewith it hath pleased God to furnish many, inabling them for publike service to their Countries both in peace and War (as all Ages and Experience testifies) on whose soules hee hath not yet pleased to shine in the face of Jesus Christ: which Gifts and Talents must all lye buried in the Earth, unlesse such persons may lawfully be called and chosen to, and improved in publike service, notwithstanding their different or contrary Conscience and Worship." [3]

In thus divorcing the ruler's calling entirely from the calling of a Christian to salvation, Williams struck at one of the springs of orthodox Puritan thinking. Puritans linked life in this world and the next by the word "calling." God called men to salvation, and He also called them to their jobs in the community where they lived. Every Puritan knew that before he undertook to be a merchant or cobbler or farmer, he must have a calling from God. A minister or magistrate must likewise be called to his office. An emigrant to New England must sense a calling to come before he boarded ship. Although the voice that called might speak only through the reason or conscience, though it might be difficult to discern, and a man might be mistaken about it, he must be sure that it was the voice of God before he could be confident that he was doing

right in hearkening to it. It must, in other words, be the
same voice that called a Christian to salvation. Every
Christian thus had two callings, usually designated as
general calling and particular calling. And in performing
the duties of his particular calling—in making his living
and serving the community—he must always subordinate
them to the duties of his general calling to serve God.[4]

The Puritans thus joined a man's every action with his
religion and laid the foundations for what a later observer
was to call "worldly asceticism." [5] Williams, in denying that
the particular calling of a ruler had anything to do with
the general calling of a Christian, was in effect denying
that the work of this world had anything to do with Christ
or Christianity. And again the observable facts seemed to
bear him out: a man could be a good shoemaker or farmer,
a good father or husband without being a Christian at all.
And conversely "a Christian Captaine, Christian Merchant,
Physitian, Lawyer, Pilot, Father, Master, and (so consequently) Magistrate, etc. is no more a Captaine, Merchant,
Physitian, Lawyer, Pilot, Father, Master, Magistrate, etc.
then [than] a Captaine, Marchant, etc. of any other Conscience or Religion." [6] The members of a community might
therefore go about their work honorably and successfully,
whatever the state of their souls. And a community in
search of a good ruler should not look simply among
Christians and neglect the talents of others who were likely
to be better qualified in the art of governing.

Even worse for the state than the withholding of political
talent was the harnessing of government to a religious
purpose. Although Williams' principal concern in the
separation of church and state was to preserve the church
from worldly contamination, he also believed that government suffered when diverted from its proper functions by
the church. Every Protestant knew how the pope had once

'corrupted the governments of Europe by making them do his bidding, and Williams could count on agreement when he reminded his readers how the pope had made dogs of "the Emperours, Kings, and Magistrates of the World, whom he teacheth and forceth to crouch, to lie downe, to creepe, and kisse his foote, and from thence at his beck to flie upon such greedie Wolves, as the Waldenses, Wicklevists, Hussites, Hugonites, Lutherans, Calvinists, Protestants, Puritans, Sectaries, etc. to imprison, to whip, to banish, to hang, to head, to burne, to blow up such vile Hereticks, Apostates, Seducers, Blasphemers etc." [7] But Williams thought that Protestants, wherever they had gained power, had done no better. Though they professed to champion the divine right of kings and governors, and even placed the government above the church, they expected the government to do what the ministers told it to do, to stamp out as heresy whatever the ministers said was heresy. And so the Protestant ministers "ride the backs and necks of Civill Magistrates, as fully and as heavily (though not so pompously) as ever the great Whore sat the backs of Popish Princes." [8] The assumption of religious purposes, then, was as bad for the state as it was for the church, because it opened the way to usurpation of civil power by the clergy, who in England, for example, had "tost up and downe (even like Tenis-bals) the Magistrates and Laws, the Consciences and Worships, the Peace and War, the Weale and Woe of this Nation." [9]

The trouble with the Puritan view as with the Catholic was that it mistook the purpose of government. Government had nothing to do with eternal salvation and only a tenuous connection with God at all. The purpose of government, said Williams, was to protect the bodies and goods of its subjects. Wherever government existed, that was the job assigned it by the people who started it. And since government could rise no higher than its source, it gained no further accretion of functions or powers if the people happened to be Christian and assigned it an authority they did not themselves possess: "that Minister or Magistrate goes beyond his commission, who intermeddles with that which cannot be given him in commission from the people." [10] Whether pagan or Christian, so long as a government protected the people who created it, in their persons and in their property, it did what a government ought to do. But when it tried to save souls, it succeeded only in injuring bodies; when it tried to protect the true church, it succeeded only in transforming true into false.

Like Machiavelli and Harrington, Williams had reached his notion of what government ought to do by asking what government can do, not merely the government of Massachusetts or of England but all governments. Simply to ask the question was to cut through a mass of casuistry and confusion, created by contending groups who saddled governments with impossible tasks and by ambitious rulers who aspired to impossible powers. To answer the question as Williams did—it was not the only possible answer—was to relieve government from the pressure of divinity and to place rulers and subjects in a new and easier relationship with each other and with other peoples.

Peace on Earth

Williams' view made all governments equal and removed the need for a government's sitting in judgment on every other government with which it might have occasion to deal. Other Puritans disagreed over the extent to which a Christian people might carry on trade or relations with infidels. In debates on the subject, expediency usually carried the day, but it had to be accompanied by extensive rationalization to make the end justify the means; and there were always disquieting voices to suggest that God's judgment might descend against a people who for any reason dealt with idolaters. John Cotton thought that Christians should not even have friends and enemies in common with them.[11] And Governor Winthrop, after assisting a neighboring Frenchman in a dispute in Nova Scotia, was told by John Endecott, the deputy governor, that Massachusetts would "have little comfort in having any thing to doe with theise Idolatrous French." Another group warned Winthrop that he might involve the colony in war and "The Ends of warre ought to be religious." [12] At the time, the continent of Europe had been engulfed for twenty-five years in the bloodiest war of its history, the ends of which were indeed religious.

Williams would have put an end to such wars. The passages of Scripture that brought on crusades against heretics and infidels were all, in his view, misapplied. Correctly understood, they instructed Christians to keep the wicked out of the church—and Williams was outdone by no one in his zeal to keep the church pure—but Christ had approved the "lawfulnesse of conversation with such persons in civill things, with whom it is not lawfull to have converse in spirituals: secretly withall foretelling, that Magistrates and People, whole States and Kingdomes should bee Idolatrous and Antichristian, yet with whom notwithstanding the Saints and Churches of God might lawfully cohabit, and hold civill converse and conversation." [13] God did not expect every people to have the same laws. With the coming of Christ, He had taken his hand from human government; and though He clearly approved government for all His creatures, He did not favor one people or one kind of government above another. As the needs and circumstances of different people varied, so must their laws and government. It was wrong, therefore, for any government to demand that another conform to its own standards.[14]

It was this attitude toward government that lent success to Williams' dealings with the Indians. He despised their religion and found many of their customs barbarous, but he was ready to live with them and deal with them on equal terms. He acknowledged each tribe as a people, and its government, however rudimentary, as equally valid and lawful with those of the English. While living in Massachusetts he got into trouble for accusing King James of having told "a solemn public lie, because in his patent he blessed God that he was the first Christian prince that had discovered this land." But Williams was less concerned with the inaccuracy of the king's claim than with the assumption underlying it: that a prince's Christianity gave him a more valid claim to the land than that enjoyed by the heathen natives. He warned the settlers that they could not really acquire land in Massachusetts by a grant from an English king: "they could have no title . . . except they compounded with the natives." [15]

More than once Williams was instrumental in preventing his fellow countrymen from going to war with the Indians over trifling causes. He did not rule out warfare altogether; he was ready to participate in the Pequot War, because it seemed clear to him that the Pequots were aggressors. But in 1640, when Massachusetts threatened a punitive war against the Niantics, Williams wrote Winthrop that even though they might deserve punishment (for the murder of a trader), "I yet doubt (now since the coming of the Lord Jesus and the period [i.e., cessation] of the National Church,) whether any other use of war and arms be lawful to the professors of the Lord Jesus, but in execution of justice upon malefactors at home: or preserving of life and lives in defensive war, as was upon the Pequots, etc. Isai. 2. Mic. 4." [16]

Williams knew that almost any war looks defensive to the people waging it, but he also knew that Europe had been drenched in blood by the aggressions of men who thought they were on some special mission for their Maker. Without denying that war might sometimes be necessary, he did deny that it could ever be holy. Since the time of Israel no people could properly claim to fight for God. There was no need to fill human disagreements with high principle. And in terms simply of the purpose of government to protect the bodies and goods of men, it was hard to see that war could be justified in any circumstance except self-defense. Again and again Williams' voice was raised for sanity against sanctity, telling his friends not to hazard life and blood for a little money, not to undertake a war that might look righteous but would end as a plague on lives and property.

The elimination of religion from government offered the prospect of peace at home as well as abroad. Protestants from the time of Luther onward had made obedience to rulers a Christian duty; but when confronted with a ruler who commanded them to be Catholics, they discovered a duty to disobey and even to overthrow. Puritan political thought had vibrated within this range, always on a religious key. It was God who demanded of every Puritan that he obey good rulers, God who demanded that he take arms against bad ones. By such reasoning, however, virtually all the governments on earth, because of their failure to uphold true religion, might have been judged unworthy of the allegiance of their subjects. All the governments of England, for example, from the rise of the papacy to the time of Henry VIII at least, must have been undeserving of support, while those from Henry VIII to Charles I could have made only doubtful claims to it. And the governments spread across the rest of the globe, whether pagan or Catholic, must be without any rightful authority at all.

The effect of giving governors holy duties, Williams saw, was to justify civil war, massacre, and assassination in the name of God. Human beings, whether Puritan, Catholic, or pagan, could always persuade themselves that God demanded the destruction of their enemies. And Puritans, who saw the hand of God in every event and sought to carry out His will in every decision, were especially susceptible to this form of self-deception. If it could be recognized that the state had less exalted purposes, that it was simply a convenient arrangement for protecting life and property, then its citizens could go about their business, including their religious business, without being obliged continually to measure the behavior of their rulers against the Word of God. Similarly if rulers went about their own limited business and stopped thinking of themselves as vicars of God, they would not give their subjects the occasion for engaging in holy rebellions.

Williams never forgot that he had been turned out of Massachusetts because the government considered his ideas seditious as well as heretical. But in his view it was the Puritan doctrine, and not his, that bred rebellion. His own ideas, he maintained, were well designed to support the authority of governments everywhere, while the Massachusetts assumption of a divine commission was calculated to overthrow every other government in the world. If the principal function of government was to avert God's wrath by enforcing His laws and especially His religion, "will it not then be unlawful for any man, that is perswaded the whole nation where he lives is idolatrous, spritually whorish, etc. I say unlawful for him to live in such a state, although he might with freedome to his own conscience? whither will such kind of arguing drive at last, but to pluck up the roots of all states and peoples in the world, as not capable to yeeld civil obedience, or exercise civil authority, except such people, Magistrates etc. as are of Master Cottons church and religion." [17]

To Williams the Puritan doctrine seemed no better than that of Cardinal Bellarmine. Indeed, Cotton and Bellarmine were "all one" in affirming the "Popish bloudy Doctrine of deposing heretical Kings." [18] Thus, in an odd alignment, Williams joined James I in linking Jesuits and Puritans together and condemning both. Not only the state but every other branch of human society must collapse if subjects were obliged to ration their obedience according to the religion of their rulers: "If this be the touchstone of all obedience, will it not be the cut-throat of all civil relations, unions and covenants between Princes and people, and between the people and people. For may not Master Cotton also say, he will not be a faithful servant, nor she a faithful wife, nor he a faithful husband, who grow false and disloyal to their God? And indeed what doth this, yea, what hath this truly-ranting doctrine (that plucks up all relations) wrought but confusion and combustion the world over?" [19]

Williams' argument against disobeying or deposing heretical rulers was in itself neither conservative nor radical; it removed the religious rationale for obedience to rulers but at the same time removed the religious rationale for rebellion. Yet Williams' intention was conservative: to eliminate civil strife and support government in carrying out its proper functions. If rulers were not God's vicegerents, if their religion had nothing to do with their fitness to rule, they could command the unquestioning obedience of all their subjects simply by virtue of the fact that they protected all their subjects' lives and property. Those conservatives who today search the American past for intellectual ancestors to make them feel at home could with some plausibility lay claim to Williams. And the American Revolutionists of 1776, though the author of their Declaration was a deist, were closer to the political ideas of orthdox Puritanism than to Williams in calling upon Nature's God to justify their resistance to tyranny. Yet to see Williams' political ideas simply as radical or conservative is to stop short of their most challenging qualities. While the very concept of a wholly prudential, secular state could have been a liberating one in Puritan thought, and proved to be so in later centuries, Williams carried the concept further than the bare denial of religious purposes and the identification of bodies and goods as the objects of governmental protection. He also considered the way government should do its job and drew some conclusions that might have troubled both radicals and conservatives of a later century.

Barbarism and Civility

The world, as Williams saw it, was divided into two sorts of men: barbarous and civil. He was ready to defend the barbarians against the pretensions of civil men who claimed superiority by virtue of their religion. But there was no doubt in his mind that civilization was preferable to barbarism. He never elaborated the differences that distinguished the two. Barbarians were simply "the wild and Pagan, whome God hath permitted to run about the world as wild Beasts," while civil men were "brought to Cloaths, to Lawes etc." [20]

Though Williams frequently added "etc." gratuitously to his phrases, this one was pregnant with implications of government. While barbarians often established loose and rudimentary governments, which must be respected, Williams generally associated government with civilization. Government was in fact the instrument by which people became or remained civil. For example, in attacking the notion that magistrates must enforce true religion or else forfeit their office, he points out that such a view would prevent most of the people of this world from forming governments and would thus force them to live as barbarians. Or again, such a view would "take away all civility." [21] In Williams' mind civility seems to have been closely associated with the rule of law and was thus dependent on government. As he at one point explained, where a magistrate fails to do justice "against scandalous offenders against civil state, that civil state must dissolve by little and little from civility to barbarisme, which is a wilderness of life and manners." [22]

Government, then, protected civility by punishing scandalous offenders against the state. Their crimes presumably violated the laws that guarded the bodies and goods of men, for Williams had ruled out the government's guardianship of men's spiritual welfare. Evidently, however, he thought that the protection of bodies and goods required the enforcement of precepts that we would describe as moral. The state, he said, must punish not only murder and theft, but also quarreling, disobedience, uncleanness, and lasciviousness, all on the grounds that they threatened the public safety.[23] If the public safety demanded that the government suppress all these, the state began to look a little less secular and not so entirely prudential as at first sight Williams had made it. The Puritan government of Massachusetts, as part of its supposed obligation to God, was suppressing precisely the same moral offenses.

To deprive government of God's assistance and to confine it to the protection of bodies and goods did not mean, for

Williams, that government had nothing to do with the moral behavior that God had prescribed for His creatures in the world. Human beings could live together happily and peaceably in "civility" only by honoring the commands which their Creator had given them. And Williams' understanding of those commands was conventional. In spite of his insistence on the merely typological significance of Israel, he believed that the coming of Christ had not abrogated the moral code delivered to Moses in the second table (commandments five through ten). This was God's revelation of "The Law of Nature, The Law Morall and Civill." [24] It was the sum of God's instructions to all men, barbarous and civil, of every nation and religion. As Creator, God did not demand one kind of moral behavior here and another there. And although the specific commands embodied in Scripture were as yet accessible only to a small part of the world, the substance of them had been discovered by peoples who had never heard of Moses or Christ and knew nothing of the way to eternal salvation. God's creatures, wherever they might live and whatever might be their destination in the world to come, had generally been able to recognize right from wrong in the affairs of this world, because God had endowed all men with conscience to guide their conduct. Said Williams, "I commend that man, whether Jew, or Turk, or Papist, or whoever, that steers no otherwise than his conscience dares." [25] If men did not in fact do what they knew to be right, it was the purpose of government to restrain them from wrong actions and constrain them to good ones, for their own safety and welfare. Where government existed, it raised men from barbarity by enforcing good morals.

In acknowledging a universal standard of morality, Williams was at one with the Puritans. He even went so far as to acknowledge that a society which wrongly attempted to enforce Christian religion might gain some incidental benefits in civility: "The Ordinances and Discipline of Christ Jesus, though wrongfully and prophanely applied to naturall and unregenerate men may cast a blush of civility and morality upon them as in Geneva and other places (for the shining brightnesse of the very shadow of Christs Ordinances casts a shame upon barbarisme and incivility)." [26]

But the fact that an affinity existed between morality and Christianity did not mean that Christians had any special talents for enforcing moral behavior. Indeed, many Christians might be less well qualified than unregenerate men. In *The Bloody Tenent yet more Bloody,* when defending the right of non-Christians to hold government office, Williams affirmed that "there is a morall vertue, a morall fidelitie, abilitie and honestie, which other men (beside Church-members) are, by good nature and education, by good Lawes and good examples nourished and trained up in, that Civill places of Trust and Credit need not to be Monopolized into the hands of Church-Members (who sometimes are not fitted for them) and all others deprived and despoiled of their naturall and Civill Rights and Liberties." [27] Here, in the very act of separating religion from government, Williams makes moral virtue a qualification for holding office and, by implication, the establishment of morality a function of government.

The establishment of morality was a function of government; the establishment of religion was not. But since morality and religion often overlapped, was it possible for a government run by men who were at least nominally Christian to enforce morality without impinging on religion? Williams thought it was, provided government paid due respect to men's consciences; and he carefully detailed what respect he thought was due.

Coercion of Conscience

Calvin had defined conscience as knowledge (*scientia*) accompanied by a sense of divine justice, and added "it is a kind of medium between God and man." [28] Before Roger Williams came to New England, two great English divines, William Perkins and William Ames, had elaborated the definition in lengthy treatises that placed conscience at the center of Puritan theology.[29] Accepting the idea that it represented the voice of God in man, they found it to be the source of natural knowledge of God's will by which man as originally created could have known what was right and wrong. Conscience was the part of man most woefully affected by Adam's fall: though not completely eradicated, it was weakened and rendered subject to error.

Since conscience was God's line of communication, a man must respect it even when it erred. It was a sin to act contrary to conscience, even a mistaken conscience. "Whatsoever man doth," said Perkins, "wherof he is not certainely perswaded in judgement and conscience out of Gods word, that the thing may be done, *it is sinne.*" And he offered as an example: "an Anabaptist, that holdeth it unlawfull to sweare, sinneth, if hee taketh an oath: not in swearing simply, for that is Gods ordinance, but because he swears against the perswasion of his conscience." [30] On the other hand, a person who violated a law of God, say by committing fornication or theft, and whose erring conscience told him these were lawful, sinned also, though not against conscience. Ames elaborated Perkins' distinction by pointing out that a man who violated God's law and whose conscience correctly informed him of the violation sinned doubly, both in the act itself and in the manner of doing it, against his conscience. A man who did what was right while erroneously thinking it wrong, sinned only in his "contempt of conscience." [31]

Although conscience was subject to error, it was also subject to correction, for God's will was made known to man not by conscience alone. God had also revealed His will in the Scriptures in order to help the weak conscience of fallen man. By close study of the Scriptures a man could test his conscience and rectify it if it conflicted with the Word. To assist the troubled consciences of men in the manifold situations of daily life, Perkins and Ames wrote their treatises. Both discussed what the conscience, when properly instructed by Scripture, must find the will of God to be in various "cases." Even an unregenerate man could benefit from such studies. Although it required the assistance of the Holy Spirit to read the full meaning of Scripture, God had given all men reason, and conscience was a function of the reason. Through the persuasive argumentation of someone who could properly explain Scripture, a man might be led to understand how his conscience erred.

Neither Ames nor Perkins gave attention to the problem of whether, if persuasion failed, coercion could make an erring conscience conform itself to God's will. Both regarded a man's conscience as something known only to the individual and to God. "God onely knowes the inward workings of the Conscience," said Ames; and Perkins stated that "mans conscience is known to none, besides himselfe, but to God." [32] It might therefore seem to follow that only God or the individual could alter the judgment of conscience. But if the inner workings of the conscience were hidden, the will of God was writ large in the Scriptures; and its applications had been spelled out by Ames and Perkins, not to mention other learned divines. Ames, therefore, after acknowledging that a man must sin in acting against an erroneous conscience, went on to eliminate the need for such an eventuality and incidentally to open a way to coercion:

Conscience through error, judging that to be lawfull *which is* unlawfull; *as that it is lawfull for one to lye, to save his owne, or his neighbours life;* bindes indeed, but *doth not bind* to do so. . . . *First, because there is no obligation to unlawfull things. Secondly, because Conscience bindeth not to do, but by vertue of some command of God; but such a conscience is not grounded upon any command: for the Law of God can neither incline nor bind any man to sinne. Thirdly, because this error is alwaies a sin, but a sin doth not bind to practice it. Fourthly, because such a Conscience hath never so sure a ground, as that there needeth not further examination and inquiry into things. Fiftly, because man is bound to lay down such a conscience; for although that be not exactly enough spoken which some do affirme, namely;* That such a Conscience bindeth a man to lay down it selfe; *yet it is most certaine, that a man is tied to lay downe such an erroneous Conscience, for it is a part of that old man, whom we are commanded to put off.* Ephes. 4.22.[33]

Ames, like many other Puritans, was a master at arriving at a desired result by making a series of distinctions. And though his distinction between conscience "binding" and "binding to do so" did not lead him to justify coercion of an erring conscience, the reasons he offers obviously point in that direction. Ames was insisting that the commands of Scripture, properly interpreted by wise and learned and saintly men, must take precedence over the erring and erratic conscience of an individual.

It was only a step from this position to that taken by the New England Puritans, and probably by most other Englishmen of the day, that a man persisting in error after being presented with persuasive arguments from Scripture was actually violating his own conscience. The will of God was not a will of the wisp, speaking different things to different men. Different men might err in discerning it, but after the truth was pointed out to them, their own consciences, however hidden from view, must indict them for error. The ministers of New England accordingly affirmed the right of the civil government there to coerce unwilling subjects, whether they pleaded conscience or not, because government "commands nothing but that which, if men have any tendernesse of conscience, they are bound in conscience to submit thereto, and in faithfull submitting to which is truest liberty of conscience, conscience being never in a truer or better estate of liberty here on earth, than when most ingaged to walke according to Gods Commandements." [34]

Williams agreed with such sentiments to a greater degree than is generally recognized. His conception of conscience was the conventional Puritan one. Conscience was "a perswasion fixed in the minde and heart of a man, which enforceth him to judge (as Paul said of himself a persecutour) and to doe so and so, with respect to God, his worship, etc." [35] Again the "etc." covered a good deal, for Williams agreed with other Puritans that conscience presided not merely over religion but over a man's whole life. This is apparent from a letter written in 1669 to a Providence neighbor, in which he defines men of conscience as "men that for fear and love of God dare not lie, nor be drunk, nor be contentious, nor steal, nor be covetous, nor voluptuous, nor ambitious, nor lazy-bodies, nor busy-bodies." [36] In 1681 Williams even lectured the citizens of Providence on their duty to pay taxes, "not only for fear, but for conscience sake." [37] Men of conscience were rare, Williams thought, but no man was without conscience. "Every savage Indian in the world" had it,[38] even though in most of the world, in the absence of the Scriptures, conscience erred freely, with small chance of correction.

Conscience was likely to err, however, even where Scripture was available. Catholics, for example, who buried the Scriptures under ceremonies and traditions, believed their erring consciences as firmly as though they were right. And Quakers, who exalted their imagined inner light above Scripture, were simply magnifying natural, unenlightened conscience. This was the gist of Willams' whole argument against them, that their neglect of Scripture and reliance on inner light was simply a stubborn insistence on following an erring conscience. And when his old friend and supporter John Endecott became governor of Massachusetts and exercised his authority in a manner that Williams thought wrong (to enforce religious conformity), Williams wrote him a long letter, explaining the error, and suggesting that if he persisted in it, now that he knew better, he would be sinning against his conscience.[39]

Not only did Williams agree with other Puritans that conscience could err and needed to be rectified by Scripture, he even advocated—up to a point—the coercion of men whose consciences erred. He affirmed the duty of the civil magistrate to punish anyone whose conscience led him to undertake actions against the public safety and welfare. And in this category he included people who conscientiously violated conventional morality. It would be proper, Williams said, for the civil government to prohibit human sacrifice, as practiced for conscience' sake in Mexico and Peru. It was also proper to prohibit prostitution, though practiced "even upon the very account of Religion and Conscience." From here he went on to approve the civil government's offering encouragement to "chastity, Humanity, etc.," and this time the "etc." included the protection of chastity by censorship of books and by proscriptions with regard to dress: "I honour," he said, "that noble act of the Emperour of Rome, who censured that famous Ovid, for that wanton Book of his *De Arte amandi,* as a sparke to immodesty and uncleanness: and doubtless it is the duty of the civil sword, to cut off the Incivilities of our times; as the monstrous haire of women, up[on] the heads of some men, etc." [40] Presumably the civil sword could be used to cut long tresses even when they were worn conscientiously, as by some Quaker men. And though he did not specifically say so, Williams doubtless thought it incumbent on government to punish those Quakers who were led by the inner light to go naked in public, a practice that deeply offended Williams and that appeared to him to be condemned even by the un-enlightened natural consciences of barbarians. The Quakers' manner of speech seemed to him to demand a "moderate restraint and punishing" because the use of the familiar "thou" to superiors savored of contempt and so violated the Fifth Commandment. The state was even entitled to punish the expression of opinions that might bring authority into contempt.[41]

Williams, then, like other Puritans, believed that government could and should coerce persons whose erring consciences led them to violate, in thought or action, the moral code of the second table. Conscience might be the medium between God and man, but conscience alone was not sufficient justification for behavior injurious to the public welfare.

Liberty of Conscience

If Williams believed that men motivated by erring consciences must be coerced, why his impassioned denunciation of "the Bloudy Tenent, of Persecution, for cause of Con-

science"? The answer is that Williams too could play the
Puritan game of making distinctions. It was not conscience
as such that he held inviolable by government, but "(meerly)
religious" conscience.[42] He thought every government was
entitled to impose a rigorous standard of behavior in matters
that affected civility, humanity, morality, or the safety of
the state and individuals in it, but no standard at all in
religion. He saw no problem in distinguishing between the
two. It was the state's job to supervise the physical behavior
of its subjects, but their spiritual lives were none of its business. When conscience (even religious conscience) led to
practices injurious to the "life, chastity, goods, or good
name" of the state's subjects, the state could legitimately
interfere to protect them.[43]

Williams acknowledged that the government would
sometimes be obliged to make nice distinctions, and he cited
some possibilities. The deciding factor in each case was
whether the outward welfare of the state and the individuals
who comprised it was involved:

*If a man call Master Cotton murtherer, witch etc. with
respect to civil matters, I say the civil state must judge and
punish the offender, else the civil state cannot stand, but
must return to barbarisme. But if a man call Master Cotton
murtherer, witch etc. in spiritual matters, as deceiving and
bewitching the peoples souls, if he can prove his charge,
Master Cotton ought to give God the glory, and repent of
such wickedness. If he cannot prove his charge, but slander
Master Cotton, yet is the slander of no civil nature, and so
not proper to any civil court, but is to be cast out (as we see
commonly suits of law are rejected, when brought into
Courts which take no proper cognizance of such cases.)* [44]

The welfare of the state also entered into Williams'
solution for dealing with Catholics, who were always feared

as a revolutionary element in Protestant countries. Since their allegiance to a foreign potentate might pose a danger to public safety, Williams suggested that they might be disarmed and required to wear distinctive clothing, but he insisted that they ought to be allowed to worship as they pleased.[45] Similarly he thought that the Quakers' contempt for authority threatened the state, and he obviously would have been happy to see them and their way of worship vanish from the face of the earth. But he called for suppression only of their "incivilities," not of their worship.

Liberty of conscience meant for Williams that no man should be prevented from worshipping as his conscience directed him. It also meant that no man should be compelled to worship against his conscience or to contribute to the support of a worship his conscience disapproved. Williams did not champion liberty of conscience in religious matters because he thought conscience was any less likely to err about religion than about other things. Indeed, it was even more likely to. While many of the principles of true morality were clear even to barbarian consciences, without benefit of Scripture, the small number of Christians in the world showed how rare it was for a conscience to be right about religion. The fallibility of conscience in this respect was for most Puritans a reason for coercing it. Williams reasoned otherwise: since the men in charge of government throughout most of the world were unlikely to be Christian and unlikely to be right themselves, they would in all probability coerce conscience the wrong way, as they had ever done in the past, to the destruction of Christ's sheep.

Even in Protestant countries and among holy men, "zealous for God and his Christ," the susceptibility to error was evident everywhere.[46] In Williams' progress from England to Massachusetts to Rhode Island he had found precious few persons whose religious consciences did not err. One need only look at the authors of the Book of Common Prayer, "in its Time, as glorious an Idoll, and as much adored by Godly persons, as any Invention now extant," yet no New Englander would have wished to have his conscience corrected by that standard.[47] The leaders of New England had themselves gained more light after their arrival in the New World; they did not accept at the beginning some of the religious ideas that prevailed later. And who was to say that they had yet arrived at truth? What now looked like perfection in Massachusetts Bay, when viewed from heaven might "look counterfeit and ugly, and be found but (spiritually) Whores and Abominations." [48]

How then could Puritan England or Scotland or Massachusetts suppress the testimony of those who "beleeve they see a further Light and dare not joyn with either of your Churches?" [49] All Protestants agreed that the Scriptures were the only source of truth about religion. Ever since the Bible had been rescued from Antichrist and restored to the people by the Reformation, it had been working a progressive enlightenment of men's consciences, revealing new and old truths to every man who searched it. But truth was not easily won, even from the Scriptures. Only by search and trial, "chewing and rational weighing and consideration" could a man arrive at a "right perswasion." [50] If in addition to the difficulties he faced from the feebleness of his own reason, he must contend with a government that forbade him to acknowledge what he found in the Scriptures, how was either he or the government to gain more light? "In vaine have English Parliaments permitted English Bibles in the poorest English houses, and the simplest man or woman to search the Scriptures, if yet against their soules perswasion from the Scripture, they should be forced (as if they lived in Spaine or Rome it selfe without the sight of a Bible) to beleeve as the Church beleeves." [51] England and New England needed all the light they could get from the Scriptures, and it might come from the simplest man or woman who read them as well as from the most learned minister. To prescribe one way of worship over another was to assume that the Scriptures had yielded all their truths infallibly to those who held the reins of power.

But even if a sure standard had existed by which to judge an erring conscience in religion, Williams thought it would be both wrong and useless to attempt to impose religious truth by force. The conscience, he was sure, could be corrected only by persuasion, and the application of force to it must have one of three effects, all bad: civil and corporal punishment might "cause men to play the hypocrite, and dissemble in their Religion, to turn and return with the tide, as all experience in the nations of the world doth testifie now"; [52] it might harden the conscience in its errors, "all false Teachers and their Followers (ordinarily) contracting a Brawnie and steelie hardnesse from their sufferings for their Consciences"; [53] or if the victim submitted and acted against his (erring) conscience, he would by so much weaken conscience itself, "since Conscience to God violated, proves (without Repentance) ever after, a very Jade, a Drug, loose and unconscionable in all converse with men." [54] Only by treating conscience tenderly, refraining from force, could it be preserved and strengthened for the future operation of Christian persuasion and the apprehension of God's truth.

All of Williams' ideas had a way of supporting one another, and his view of the change wrought in history by the coming of Christ strengthened his certainty that force must not be used against any man's conscience in religious matters. Since the downfall of Israel, the only true religion was that of a Saviour who forswore the use of force. By the very attempt to coerce conscience a magistrate demonstrated that the religion he was enforcing was not Christian. It was "impossible for any Man or Men to maintaine their Christ by their Sword, and to worship a true Christ!" [55]

But if government could do nothing with its whips and scourges and prisons to make men Christian, Williams did not deny it all opportunity to advance Christ's kingdom. There was one thing government could do, though few governments had ever done it: government could protect the free exercise of conscience in religion.[56] Any government that properly fulfilled its obligation to guard without discrimination the bodies and goods of all its subjects would automatically achieve this end. But it required a vigilance and impartiality that were rare among rulers to watch over the exercise of religion in such a way as to prevent one group within the state from usurping authority over the consciences of other groups. When priests rode the backs of kings, government could not fulfill this obligation. Sometimes, to be sure, a government would throw off these tyrants of the soul and strike a blow for freedom of conscience. Williams sang the praises of the English Parliament for "breaking the jaws of the oppressing Bishops," but he was saddened by the prospect that the same Parliament would blemish its record "by erecting in their stead a more refined, but yet as cruel an Episcopacy." [57] Parliament had failed to learn that one religious belief could be favored above another only at the expense of truth. The Christian magistrate could best advance the cause of his own religion by doing it no favors.

If a civil magistrate was a Christian, he must, as an individual, submit his own soul to the spiritual government of Christ, but as a magistrate he owed the same protection to false religion as he did to his own. Williams asserted,

THE BUSINESS OF GOVERNMENT

in other words, the right of a man to be wrong about religion and to be protected in his error by the civil government. He was by no means the first Puritan to defend "liberty of conscience," but other Puritans, though admitting that a man sinned in acting against an erring conscience, were prepared to impose this sin upon him. The only liberty they allowed was a liberty to do right, and they demanded that government coerce men whose consciences led them astray, whether in morals or religion.[58] Williams agreed as far as morals were concerned (though some of his arguments could have been applied here, he did not apply them), but in religion, the matter about which he and his contemporaries cared most, he defined liberty of conscience as the right to be wrong.

Williams' defense of liberty of conscience would seem to have been somewhat more limited than that which a Thomas Jefferson or a James Madison offered in the next century. Though Williams honored conscience in any form, he had sworn eternal warfare not against every tyranny over the mind of man but only against compulsion in religion. With a low opinion of the efficacy of human reason, his goal was not freedom of thought for its own sake: he did not think that one way of seeking God was as good as another. He wanted freedom because it was the only way to reach the true God. Although few men would reach Him at best, only freedom of conscience could bring them to Him, because Christ had forsworn the use of force. And history had demonstrated, to Williams at least, that force always favored false religion.

But the difference between Williams' view and that which ultimately prevailed in the United States is easily exaggerated. If Williams had little confidence in human reason, this fact did not separate him as far from the Founding Fathers of the United States as might at first appear. Their confidence in reason also had its limits; in framing the Constitution they tried to guard the nation against the fallibility of its own citizens. And if Williams demanded freedom of conscience because Christ demanded it, this was his way of saying what every eighteenth-century philosopher would have applauded, that the free exercise of reason is the only way to truth. The conscience, for Williams, belonged to the reason, and in vindicating it he was vindicating reason—reason corrupted by the fall of man, reason needing the aid of Scripture and of saving grace, but reason nonetheless.

It does not follow that we should give Williams back to the nineteenth- and twentieth-century liberals who have claimed him for their own. Williams belonged to the seventeenth century, to Puritanism and to Separatism. What he did share with a number of men, in his own century as well as before and since, was a quality that always seems to lift a man above his time: intellectual courage, the willingness to go where the mind leads. When his mind told him there could be no church, he left the church, even though he wanted nothing more than to serve it. When his mind told him the state could do nothing but harm to religion, he said so, even though it cost him everything he had. We may praise him (and so ourselves) for his defense of religious liberty and the separation of church and state. He deserves the tribute (and so perhaps do we?). But it falls short of the man. His greatness was simpler. He dared to think.

Notes
Index

Notes to Chapter I

1. *The Complete Writings* (7 vols., New York, 1963), VI, 228.

2. The most thorough, scholarly biographies of Williams are Samuel H. Brockunier, *The Irrepressible Democrat* (New York, 1940) and Ola E. Winslow, *Master Roger Williams* (New York, 1957).

3. The edition I have used is *The Complete Writings* (abbreviated hereafter as *CW*) published by Russell and Russell (New York, 1963), the first six volumes of which are simply facsimiles of the volumes edited for the Narragansett Club by James Hammond Trumbull, Reuben Aldridge Guild, J. Lewis Diman, Samuel L. Caldwell, and John Russell Bartlett. These were published between 1866 and 1874. The seventh volume of *CW*, edited by Perry Miller, consists of tracts that were not included by the Narragansett Club. The only serious omission in *CW* is in the sixth volume, containing Williams' letters. This has not been brought up to date by the inclusion of a number of letters that have come to light and been published since 1874. The most important of these are to be found in Massachusetts Historical Society, *Proceedings*, new series, III (1886–87), 256–259; *Rhode Island Historical Tracts*, No. 14 (1881), 25–62; Rhode Island Historical Society, *Publications*, new series, VIII (1900), 141–161; Rhode Island Historical Society, *Proceedings*, for 1883–84, 79–81; and *New England Historic Genealogical Register*, XLIII (1889), 315–320. Photostats of most of the extant letters, compiled by Howard M. Chapin, were published by the Massachusetts Historical Society in 1924.

In citations to *CW* I have not identified the titles of the tracts referred to. Anyone may do so from the following table:

CW, I,	77–282	*A Key into the Language of America* (1643)
	295–311	John Cotton, *A Letter of Mr. John Cottons* (1643)
	313–396	*Mr Cottons Letter Lately Printed, Examined and Answered* (1644)

CW, II,   9–237   John Cotton, *A Reply to Mr Williams his
                            Examination and Answer of the Letters sent to
                            him by John Cotton* (1647)
                 251–275   *Queries of Highest Consideration* (1644)

CW, III,   1–425   *The Bloudy Tenent, of Persecution, for cause
                            of Conscience, discussed, in A Conference
                            betweene Truth and Peace* (1644)

CW, IV,   1–547   *The Bloody Tenent yet more Bloody: By Mr
                            Cottons endevour to wash it white in the Blood
                            of the Lambe* (1652)

CW, V,   1–503   *George Fox Digg'd out of his Burrowes* (1676)

CW, VI,   1–408   Letters (1632–82)

CW, VII,   29–41   *Christenings make not Christians* (1645)
                  45–114   *Experiments of Spiritual Life and Health* (1652)
                 119–141   *The Fourth Paper, Presented by Major Butler
                            . . . together with a Testimony to the said
                            fourth Paper* (1652)
                 147–191   *The Hireling Ministry None of Christs* (1652)
                 195–279   *The Examiner Defended* (1652)

In transcribing quotations I have eliminated italics, which
Williams used so generously as to destroy whatever emphasis
he may have intended.

4. John Winthrop's *Journal* (published, in the best edition,
as *The History of New England*, James Savage, ed., 2 vols.,
Boston 1853. Hereafter, *Journal*) is almost the only contemporary source.

5. Brockunier, *Irrepressible Democrat*, 3–40; Winslow,
Williams, 1–94.

6. In this and the next four paragraphs I am deeply indebted to William Haller, *The Elect Nation: The Meaning and
Relevance of Foxe's Book of Martyrs* (New York, 1963). I am
also indebted to Joy Bourne Gilsdorf, The Puritan Apocalypse: New England Eschatology in the Seventeenth Century.
Unpublished doctoral dissertation (1964), Yale University.

7. Haller, *Elect Nation*, 87.

8. *CW*, IV, 442; see also IV, 384; III, 184.

9. Charles H. and Katherine George, *The Protestant Mind of the English Reformation, 1570–1640* (Princeton, 1961). For an opposing view see John F. H. New, *Anglican and Puritan: The Basis of Their Opposition, 1558–1640* (Stanford, California, 1964).

10. E. S. Morgan, *Visible Saints: The History of a Puritan Idea* (New York, 1963), 66–73. For a full discussion of the early stages of conversion, in which unaided human efforts played a large role, see Norman Pettit, *The Heart Prepared* (New Haven, 1966).

11. For example, William Perkins (1558–1602) and John Preston (1587–1628).

12. (London, 1652), *CW*, VII, 42–114.

13. The classic scholarly exposition is Perry Miller, "The Marrow of Puritan Divinity," Colonial Society of Massachusetts, *Publications*, XXXII (1937), 247–300, reprinted in Miller, *Errand into the Wilderness* (Cambridge, Mass., 1956), 48–98. The ramifications of the concept are discussed at length in Miller, *The New England Mind: The Seventeenth Century* (New York, 1939), 365–491.

14. See his exposition of it, *CW*, V, 331–334.

15. Miller, *New England Mind*, 432–462. See also in general: Miller, *Orthodoxy in Massachusetts* (Cambridge, Mass., 1933); Williston Walker, *Creeds and Platforms of Congregationalism* (New York, 1893); Champlin Burrage, *The Church Covenant Idea* (Philadelphia, 1904).

16. Miller, *Orthodoxy in Massachusetts*, 73–101.

17. *A Necessitie of Separation from the Church of England, proved by the Nonconformists Principles* ([Amsterdam], 1634). Reprinted, London, 1849, Charles Stovel, ed.

18. *CW*, I, 381.

19. See Morgan, *Visible Saints*, 20–63, for a fuller description and documentation of the Separatist view of the Church of England and of the distinguishing marks of a true church.

20. John Robinson, *Works*, Robert Ashton, ed. (3 vols., Boston, 1851), II, 60; cf. Canne, *Necessitie of Separation*, 155–163.

21. Champlin Burrage, *The Early English Dissenters in the Light of Recent Research* (2 vols., Cambridge, England. 1912), II, 13–15.

22. 2 Cor. 6. 17.

23. John Smyth, *Parallels, Censures, Observations* ([Amsterdam], 1609), 111; Henry Barrow, *A Collection of Certain Letters* ([Dort], 1590), 59.

24. Robinson, *Works*, III, 363.

25. *Ibid.*

26. Morgan, *Visible Saints*, 64–112.

27. *CW*, VI, 356.

28. *Journal*, I, 63.

29. *Ibid.*

30. *CW*, VI, 356; William Bradford, *History of Plymouth Plantation* (2 vols., Boston, 1912), II, 161–164.

31. *CW*, I, 378. John Cotton asserted in 1647: "It was well knowne that whilest he lived at Salem, he neither admitted, nor permitted any Church-members, but such as rejected all Communion with the Parish Assemblies, so much as in hearing of the Word amongst them" (*ibid.* II, 106).

32. *Journal*, I, 210; cf. *CW*, I, 325.

33. E. S. Morgan, *The Puritan Dilemma* (Boston, 1958), 115–133.

Notes to Chapter II

1. Typical examples of the metaphor will be found in *CW*, I, 392; III, 95, 184, 415.

2. *CW*, IV, 336–337.

3. *CW*, III, 133–134, 184; IV, 147, 442. The importance Williams attached to words is suggested by a story of Cotton Mather's, possibly apocryphal but plausible. While Williams was at Plymouth, Mather says, he embroiled the church in a dispute by insisting that the common English designations for persons of yeoman status, "goodman" and "goodwife," must be used only for the regenerate, since they alone were truly good. *Magnalia Christi Americana* (London, 1702), Book II, 13.

4. *CW*, VII, 26–41; cf. *CW*, IV, 368–374.

5. He mentions writing it in a letter to John Winthrop, *CW*, VI, 50.

6. *CW*, III, 203; cf. *CW*, I, 389.

7. *CW*, II, 272; cf. *CW*, I, 384–389; III, 234, 290.

8. For example John Canne, in *A Stay Against Straying* ([Amsterdam], 1639). But Canne believed that while true Christians must not participate in hearing Anglican preachers, there was "no daunger" in letting "an Heretick, Atheist or whatsoever" attend the preaching of the Word in a true Christian church (pp. 9–10).

9. *Journal*, I, 194.

10. Winthrop recorded this as Williams' opinion in 1635 (*Journal*, I, 194), and Williams himself recalled among the accusations made against him in Massachusetts his statement that "it is not lawfull to call a wicked Person to Sweare, to Pray, as being actions of Gods Worship." Williams acknowleged the accuracy of the charge (*CW*, I, 325).

11. *CW*, VII, 188.

12. *CW*, III, 138.

13. *CW*, III, 225.

14. Morgan, *Visible Saints*, 64–112.

15. *CW*, V, 103; cf. *CW*, I, 350.

16. Morgan, *Visible Saints*, 64–112; Burrage, *Early English Dissenters*, II, 13–15.

17. *CW*, I, 363.

18. *CW*, I, 350.

19. *CW*, I, 348; cf. *CW*, I, 352, 356–358, 366; II, 102.

20. *CW*, I, 348–349.

21. *CW*, IV, 205.

22. *CW*, I, 348–349, 352; IV, 270–271.

23. *CW*, II, 272–273.

24. *Journal*, I, 352–353.

25. *Ibid.*, I, 369.

26. *CW*, I, 329–330.

27. *CW*, III, 289.

28. *CW*, I, 387; cf. *CW*, IV, 132.

29. *CW*, I, 387.

30. *CW*, V, 120–121.

31. *CW*, II, 212.

32. *CW*, III, 302; VII, 176.

33. *CW*, VI, 2.

34. *Rhode Island Historical Tracts*, No. 14 (1881), 53.

35. *Journal*, I, 369.

36. *CW*, VII, 162.

37. *CW*, VII, 160.

38. John Foxe maintained that after the triumph of Antichrist, the church "durst not openly appear in the face of the world . . . yet neither was it so invisible or unknown, but, by the providence of the Lord, some remnant always remained from time to time, which not only showed secret good affection to sincere doctrine, but also stood in open defiance against the disordered church of Rome." John Foxe, *Actes and Monuments of these latter and perillous dayes*, S. R. Cattley, ed. (8 vols., London, 1841), I, 517. Cf. John Cotton's similar view in *CW*, II, 72–73, 112–114.

39. It was the duty of believers to form churches or to join churches already formed. If they neglected this duty, the ministers of New England pointed out in 1648, "it might follow thereupon, that Christ should have no visible political churches upon earth" (Walker, *Creeds and Platforms,* 209).

40. William Perkins, *Workes* (3 vols., London, 1626–31), II, 172.

41. *Works*, II, 147–148, 418–450. Robinson would have agreed with Williams that the apostolic succession had been broken, but he denied that this extinguished the church.

42. Miller, *Orthodoxy in Massachusetts*, 88–90, 152–154.

43. Walker, *Creeds and Platforms*, 210, 215.

44. *Ibid.*, 216.

45. New Englanders nevertheless worried about the validity of laymen creating a minister. Whenever possible, they maintained, the laying on of hands should be performed by neighboring ministers. In the eighteenth century many New Englanders who otherwise revered the doctrines of their ancestors re-

pudiated lay ordination altogether and insisted that the ministerial office could not be properly conveyed except by another minister, one who could trace his own ordination back through a succession of other ministers to Christ and the apostles.

46. These views are implicit wherever Williams discusses the church. Occasionally they become explicit, as in the following passage: ". . . we find not in the first institution and patterne [of the church], that ever any such two, or three, or more, did gather and constitute themselves a church of Christ, without a Ministrie sent from God to invite and call them by the Word, and to receive them unto fellowship with God upon the receiving of that Word and Message: And therefore it may very well be quaeried how without such a Ministry two or three become a Church? and how the power of Christ is conveyed unto them; Who espoused this people unto Jesus Christ, as the Church at Corinth was espoused by Paul, 2 Cor. 11? If it be said themselves, or if it be said the Scriptures, let one instance be produced in the first patternes and practices of such a Practice" (*CW*, III, 293–294).

47. *CW*, III, 296–297.

48. *CW*, VII, 131.

49. *CW*, VII, 159–160.

50. *CW*, VII, 175–176.

51. *CW*, I, 352; cf. *CW*, IV, 383.

52. *CW*, IV, 368–374.

53. When Williams returned to Salem from Plymouth in 1633, Samuel Skelton was pastor there and Williams apparently was not chosen to any formal office in the church. Skelton died in August, 1634, and in December of that year one James Cudworth, listing the churches and ministers of the colony, said that "at Salem theare Pastor old Mr. Skelton is ded: theare is Mr. Williams who Doe exercise his giftes but is in no office" (letter to Dr. Stoughton, British Public Record Office. C.O. 1/8, 110–111 ff.). But in July, 1635, when Williams was in trouble with the General Court, Winthrop observed that Salem "had chosen Mr. Williams their teacher, while he stood under question of authority, and so offered contempt to the

magistrates" (*Journal,* I, 195). The next month Winthrop referred to Williams as "pastor of Salem" (*ibid.,* I, 198). When
a church had only one minister, the question whether he was
pastor or teacher was of no great consequence. John Cotton
in 1648 stated that Williams had been teacher of the Salem
church. According to Cotton, Williams had once said that "of
all the Churches in the world, the Churches of New-England
are the most pure, and of all New-English churches, Salem
(wherof himself was Teacher) was the purest" (*The Way of
the Congregational Churches Cleared,* London, 1648, 28).

    54. *Winthrop Papers* (Boston, 1929–   ), III (1943), 11.

    55. Robert Baillie, *Letters and Journals,* David Laing, ed.
(3 vols., Edinburgh, 1841–42), II, 191, 212.

    56. It has been common, especially since the articles and
biographies of James Ernst, to label Williams as a Seeker
("Roger Williams and the English Revolution," Rhode Island
Historical Society, *Collections,* XXIV [1931], 1–58, 118–128;
Roger Williams, New England Firebrand, New York, 1932).
Nowhere in Williams' own writings have I found the word
used or any evidence that Williams knew or corresponded
with English Seekers. The only contemporary attribution that
I have seen connecting him with them (unless the statement
by Baillie may be counted as such) is one quoted by Ernst,
in which Henry Nicolls, a Welsh minister, refers to Williams
as having taught one Master Erbury (Rhode Island Historical
Society, *Collections,* XXIV, 8). Erbury, who was usually called
a Seeker, did believe that existing churches were false, but in
all other respects his views were quite contrary to those of
Williams. (See Thomas Edwards, *Gangraena,* London, 1646,
Part I, 77–78; Part III, 89–90; [Francis Cheynell], *An Account
Given to the Parliament,* London, 1646.) According to Ernst,
Richard Baxter also spoke of Williams as "the father of the
Seekers of London," (Rhode Island Historical Society, *Collec-
tions,* XXIV, 6) but in the citation given (to *Reliquiae
Baxterianae* [London, 1696], Part I, 76) Baxter does not mention
Williams and says merely that "the Papists principally hatcht
and actuated" the Seekers and that they were later identified

with the "Vanists," that is, the Antinomian followers of Henry Vane.

57. *CW*, I, 350; V, 103. But he told John Winthrop, Jr. in 1649 of a number of Baptists at Providence who rebaptized by dipping, and added, "I believe their practice comes nearer the first practice of our great Founder Christ Jesus, then other practices of religion do, and yet I have not satisfaction neither in the authority by which it is done, nor in the manner" (*CW*, VI, 188).

58. *CW*, III, 293.

59. *CW*, I, 388.

60. *CW*, III, 403.

61. *CW*, VII, 40-41.

62. *CW*, IV, 201-202; cf. *CW*, V, 102.

63. *CW*, VI, 311; cf. *CW*, VI, 307-308.

64. *CW*, I, 382.

65. *CW*, V, 205.

66. *CW*, V, 418.

67. *CW*, V, 386; cf. *CW*, V, 101-103, 165, 260, 340-341.

68. *CW*, V, 234.

69. *CW*, V, 260-261.

70. *CW*, V, 418-419.

Notes to Chapter III

1. J. N. Figgis, *The Divine Right of Kings* (Cambridge, England, 1896; New York, 1965); C. H. McIlwain, *The Political Works of James I* (Cambridge, Mass., 1918).

2. For characteristic statements of the Puritan view by men who later enjoyed a high reputation in New England, see William Perkins, *Workes*, I, 194; III, 503, 536, 538; William Bradshaw, *English Puritanism* ([London], 1640 [written in 1605]), 7, 10, 15, 22, 27, 29-30; William Ames, *The Marrow of Sacred Divinity* (London, [1642]), 167, 313-314; Henry Burton, *The Baiting of the Pope's Bull* (London, 1627), 50-52.

3. Burton, *Baiting of the Pope's Bull*, 51.

4. Bradshaw, *English Puritanism,* 15, 30. The differences between Congregational and Presbyterian Puritans were not as clear before 1630 as they later became, but it is already possible in the writings of such men as Ames, Bradshaw, and Burton to recognize the outlines of the later Congregational polity. These men placed all churches and ministers on an equal footing, "none above another," and from this position it was easy to add "much lesse above others [i.e., above kings or rulers] in any Temporall Jurisdiction" (Burton, *Baiting of the Pope's Bull,* 52. Cf. Ames, *Marrow,* 145).

5. W. S. Holdsworth, *A History of English Law* (13 vols., London, 1922–52), I, 580–632.

6. *Ibid.*

7. Wallace Notestein, *The English People on the Eve of Colonization, 1603–1630* (New York, 1954), 240–249; Sedley Ware, *The Elizabethan Parish in its Ecclesiastical and Financial Aspects* (Baltimore, 1908); Mildred Campbell, *The English Yeoman under Elizabeth and the Early Stuarts* (New Haven, 1942), Ch. IX.

8. Walker, *Creeds and Platforms,* 227–229; Thomas Hooker, *A Survey of the Summe of Church Discipline* (London, 1648), Part III, 33–46; John Cotton, *The Way of the Churches of Christ in New England* (London, 1645), 13–38.

9. N. B. Shurtleff, ed., *Records of the Governor and Company of the Massachusetts Bay* (5 vols. in 6, Boston, 1853–54), I, 242 (Sept. 6, 1638).

10. *Ibid.,* I, 246, 271. The law was repealed September 4, 1639.

11. W. H. Whitmore, ed., *The Colonial Laws of Massachusetts. Reprinted from the Edition of 1660 . . . containing also, The Body of Liberties of 1641* (Boston, 1889), 46.

12. *Records of Mass. Bay,* III, 3, 5.

13. Winthrop, *Journal,* I, 97.

14. *Ibid.,* I, 344; cf. II, 228.

15. Whitmore, *Colonial Laws,* 172, 200–201; Thomas E. Atkinson, "The Development of the Massachusetts Probate System," *Michigan Law Review,* XLII (1943), 425–452; G. L.

Haskins, *Law and Authority in Early Massachusetts* (New York, 1960), 183–185, 194–195.

16. The magistrates were suspicious of Hobart anyhow because of his leanings toward Presbyterianism. Winthrop, *Journal*, II, 382.

17. *Records of Mass. Bay*, I, 252.

18. Winthrop, *Journal*, I, 255.

19. *Ibid.*, I, 331.

20. *Records of Mass. Bay*, I, 274–275.

21. The word "elders," though capable of extension to include ruling elders, normally signified the ordained pastors and teachers of the churches.

22. *Journal*, II, 19–20.

23. *Ibid.*, II, 46–48.

24. *Ibid.*, I, 255.

25. See Bradshaw, *English Puritanism*, 29; Henry Barrowe, *A Brief Discoverie of the False Church* [Dort, 1590], 246–247.

26. *Journal*, I, 300; *Winthrop Papers*, III, 505–507.

27. Whitmore, *Colonial Laws*, 57.

28. *Records of Mass. Bay*, I, 82.

29. *Ibid.*, I, 140, 216–217, 240; American Antiquarian Society, *Proceedings*, new series, IV (1885–87), 107–109

30. *Journal*, I, 355.

31. *Records of Mass. Bay*, I, 87.

32. Thomas Hutchinson, *The History of the Colony and Province of Massachusetts Bay*, L. S. Mayo, ed. (3 vols., Cambridge, Mass., 1936), I, 414–417.

33. *Journal*, II, 3–4.

34. *Ibid.*, II, 154.

35. *Ibid.*, II, 140.

36. *Winthrop Papers*, IV, 491–493.

37. *Journal*, I, 390–392. The General Court for a time tried to regulate the hour when lectures were given but also gave this up. *Records of Mass. Bay*, I, 109–110, 290.

38. Robert Gray, *An Alarum to England* (London, 1609), no pagination.

39. Morgan, *Puritan Dilemma*, 18–44.

40. Bradford, *Plymouth Plantation*, I, 3; Edward Winslow, *Hypocrisie Unmasked* (London, 1646), 89.

41. William L. Sachse, "The Migration of New Englanders to England, 1640–1660," *American Historical Review*, LIII (1948), 251–278; "Harvard Men in England, 1642–1714," Colonial Society of Massachusetts, *Publications*, XXXV (1942–46), 119–144.

42. *Winthrop Papers*, II, 293–294.

43. Miller, *New England Mind*, 398–431; Morgan, *Puritan Dilemma, passim*. On Puritan historians, see Perry Miller and Thomas Johnson, eds., *The Puritans* (New York, 1938), 81–90; K. B. Murdock, *Literature and Theology in Colonial New England* (Cambridge, Mass., 1949), 67–97; and Peter Gay, *A Loss of Mastery: Puritan Historians in Colonial America* (Berkeley, Calif., 1966).

44. *Records of Mass. Bay*, V, 59–63.

45. *Ibid.*, V, 59.

Notes to Chapter IV

1. Perry Miller, *Roger Williams: His Contribution to the American Tradition* (New York and Indianapolis, 1953), 27.

2. *CW*, V, 331–334.

3. Miller, *New England Mind*, 365–491; E. S. Morgan, ed. *Puritan Political Ideas* (Indianapolis, 1965), *passim.*, esp. xx-xxv, 261–262.

4. *CW*, IV, 282.

5. Walker, *Creeds and Platforms*, 47, 71, 80; Miller, *Orthodoxy in Massachusetts*, 61–66.

6. *Journal*, I, 63.

7. The pervasive influence of typology in Williams' thought is demonstrated in Perry Miller, *Roger Williams,* and in Miller's introduction to Volume VII of *CW* (5–25). Professor Jesper Rosenmeier, of Tufts University, has discussed the difference between Williams' and Cotton's use of typology in "The Teacher and the Witness: John Cotton and Roger Williams," an un-

published essay which Professor Rosenmeier kindly allowed me to read.

8. Throughout his writings Williams habitually used this cryptic phrase, from Revelation I. 16, to designate the purely spiritual powers of the church.

9. Williams did not specifically deny that the temple was a type of the church, but he seems to have been unique, among American Puritans at least, in maintaining that the type of the church was Israel itself.

10. *CW*, IV, 28–29; cf. *CW*, III, 369.

11. *CW*, III, 214.

12. *CW*, III, 250; cf. *CW*, III, 355–356; IV, 210.

13. *The Bloudy Tenent, washed, And made white in the bloud of the Lambe* (London, 1647), 101–102.

14. *CW*, IV, 193.

15. *CW*, IV, 244; cf. *CW*, IV, 165, 193.

16. *CW*, IV, 442; cf. *CW*, III, 184; IV, 384.

17. *CW*, III, 143.

18. *CW*, IV, 389.

19. *CW*, I, 327.

20. *CW*, I, 326–327; IV, 253, 301–304, 389–390.

21. *The Bloudy Tenent, washed,* 95.

22. *CW*, III, 325–326; cf. *CW*, II, 259–260; III, 136–137; VII, 205.

23. *CW*, IV, 204.

24. *CW*, III, 137, 326.

25. *CW*, VII, 225–226. John Lambert was burned at the stake in 1538 for holding views of the sacrament unacceptable to Henry VIII.

26. *CW*, VII, 29–41; cf. *CW*, VI, 191, 193, 198.

27. *CW*, IV, 488; cf. *CW*, VI, 191, 193, 198.

28. *CW*, IV, 484–488.

29. *CW*, III, 145–146.

30. *CW*, IV, 71.

31. *CW*, IV, 188; cf. *CW*, IV, 403–404.

32. *CW*, VII, 248–250.

33. For other examples of his inconsistent employment of

the concept against his opponents, see *CW*, I, 340, 361; II, 268; III, 419; IV, 179, 189; V, 364; VI, 402; VII, 186.

34. *CW*, IV, 208–209.

35. *CW*, IV, 206.

36. *CW*, VI, 319.

37. *CW*, VII, 248.

38. For typical Puritan statements on the perils of prosperity and the advantages of adversity, see William Perkins, *Workes*, II, 29–39; III, 141, 183–193; John Downame, *A Guide to Godlynesse* (London, 1622), 343–363.

39. *CW*, VII, 53.

40. *CW*, VII, 215. In 1652, with Oliver Cromwell in control in England, Williams seems for a time to have thought that God might have singled out England as an example and precedent for the rest of the world. See *CW*, VII, 186. This view was of course not entirely consistent with his insistence that God had favored no nation since Israel.

41. *CW*, VII, 215; cf. *CW*, II, 270–271; III, 189, 244, 284–285; VII, 215–216.

42. *CW*, IV, 404.

43. *CW*, I, 298–299.

44. *CW*, I, 340, 342.

45. *CW*, VII, 224.

46. *CW*, IV, 381.

47. *CW*, IV, 303.

48. *Ibid.*

49. *CW*, III, 304–305; cf. *CW*, III, 298.

50. *CW*, VII, 164–165.

51. *CW*, VII, 152.

52. *CW*, VII, 172.

53. *CW*, VII, 170.

54. *CW*, III, 305–308.

55. *CW*, III, 359.

56. *CW*, IV, 243.

57. Increase Mather, *A Discourse Concerning the Danger of Apostacy* (Boston, 1679), 111.

Notes to Chapter V

1. G. L. Mosse, *The Holy Pretence: A Study in Christianity and Reason of State from William Perkins to John Winthrop* (Oxford, 1957).

2. *CW*, III, 414.

3. *CW*, III, 331; cf. *CW*, III, 355.

4. E. S. Morgan, *The Puritan Family* (New York, 1966), 68–78.

5. Max Weber, *The Protestant Ethic and the Spirit of Capitalism* (New York, 1958), 95–154.

6. *CW*, III, 398–399.

7. *CW*, IV, 430.

8. *CW*, IV, 430; cf. *CW*, IV, 361–362.

9. *CW*, VII, 189–190.

10. *CW*, IV, 187.

11. *CW*, II, 226.

12. *Winthrop Papers*, IV, 394, 400.

13. *CW*, III, 117.

14. *CW*, III, 364; IV, 485.

15. Winthrop, *Journal*, I, 145.

16. *CW*, VI, 139.

17. *CW*, IV, 242; cf. *CW*, IV, 238.

18. *CW*, IV, 281; cf. *CW*, IV, 205–206, 420.

19. *CW*, IV, 207; cf. *CW*, III, 331–332, 415.

20. *CW*, V, 258. The distinction was, of course, not original with Williams. It is assumed, again without elaboration, in much of the earliest English discussion of colonization. See, for example, D. B. Quinn, ed., *The Voyages and Colonizing Enterprises of Sir Humphrey Gilbert* (2 vols., London, 1940), Works issued by the Hakluyt Society, second series, LXXXIII and LXXXIV, 125–126, 160–161, 181, 357, 361, 434–482.

21. *CW*, III, 201; VII, 236.

22. *CW*, IV, 222.

23. *CW*, III, 108–109.

24. *CW*, III, 358.

25. *CW*, VI, 328.

26. *CW*, III, 225.

27. *CW*, IV, 365.

28. *Institutes of the Christian Religion*, John Allen, trans. (2 vols., Philadelphia, 1932), II, 75.

29. William Perkins, *The Whole Treatise of the Cases of Conscience*, in *Workes*, II, 1–152; William Ames, *Conscience, with the Power and Cases Thereof, Divided into five Bookes*, in *Workes* (London, 1643), separate pagination.

30. Perkins, *Workes*, II, 12.

31. Ames, *Conscience*, Book I, 9.

32. *Ibid.*, Book I, 5; Perkins, *Workes*, II, 11.

33. Ames, *Conscience*, Book I, 9–10.

34. Walker, *Creeds and Platforms*, 190.

35. *CW*, IV, 508.

36. *CW*, VI, 329.

37. *CW*, VI, 402.

38. *CW*, V, 443; cf. IV, 508–509.

39. *CW*, IV, 506–507.

40. *CW*, VII, 243.

41. *CW*, V, 58–62, 306–308; VII, 179–180.

42. *CW*, VII, 179.

43. *CW*, III, 171.

44. *CW*, IV, 148.

45. *CW*, IV, 313–314.

46. *CW*, IV, 510.

47. *Ibid.*

48. *CW*, IV, 511.

49. *CW*, II, 273.

50. *CW*, III, 13; V, 292.

51. *CW*, III, 13.

52. *CW*, IV, 209.

53. *CW*, IV, 496; cf. *CW*, III, 272-273.

54. *CW*, IV, 498–499.

55. *CW*, IV, 515.

56. *CW*, III, 129; VII, 178–187.

57. *CW*, IV, 195.

58. Williams' friend John Winthrop, for example, insisted that the liberty enjoyed by men in civil society was a liberty "to that only which is good, just, and honest" (*Journal*, II, 281).

Index

extinction of church, 55; pamphlet against, 57; on support of ministry, 75, 111; on church and state, 76, 95, 98; on Williams' sickness, 109; on relations with idolaters, 121; and tyrannicide, 125; and coercion of conscience, 136

Covenant: national, 8; of works, 13; of redemption, 13–14; of grace, 13–16; political, 14–15, 87–90; church, 15–16, 19–20, 37, 47–49

Covenant theology, 13–17

Cromwell, Oliver, 31, 56, 80, 158

Cudworth, James, 151

David, 108

Depravity, 11–12, 59–60, 95

Discipline, *see* Church discipline

Divorce, 67, 71

Dudley, Thomas, 77–78

Edward VI, 18

Edwards, Jonathan, 32

Egypt, 105

Election sermons, 77

Elizabeth I, 6–10, 18, 100

Endecott, John, 121, 134

England: place in history, 6–10; as successor of Israel, 14–15, 80, 99–102; Williams in, 53, 90; church and state in, 64, 66–67

Ernst, James, 152

Evangelists, 43, 44

Excommunication, 19–20, 67, 69–70; *see also* Church discipline

Fasting, 82

First Amendment, 62

Fox, George, 57–61

Foxe, John, 8, 150

Freedom of religion, *see* Conscience

Freedom of speech, 63, 73, 135, 136

Garden, as image of church, 28, 30, 38, 96

Geneva, 129

George III, 114

Gloucester, Mass., 70

God: Williams' view of, 49, 54, 58, 88–89; wrath of, 80–84, 103–108, 114, 121

Gomorrha, 80, 103

Government: art of, 115–120; purpose of, 118–120; and war, 120–123; and rebellion, 123–126; and civility, 126–129; and morality, 127–135; and public welfare, 127–128, 134–135, 136–137; and coercion of conscience, 130–135; and liberty of conscience, 135–142; *see also* State

Gray, Robert, 80

Harrington, James, 115, 120

Henry VIII, 18, 100, 101, 123

Heresy, 72, 84, 98, 119, 123–125

excommunication in, 69–
70; religious qualification
for office in, 70–71, 76, 117;
sumptuary laws of, 72–73;
influence of ministers in,
76–79; as successor of Israel,
81–84, 102–103, 112–113
Mather, Cotton, 148–149
Mather, Increase, 113–114
Mexico, 134
Millennium, 9
Miller, Perry, 86
Ministry: among Separatists,
21–22; pastoral and apos-
tolic, 40–46; extinction of,
45–46; and Christ's commission, 46–50, 54–56; ordination of, 47–48; of prophets
in sackcloth, 50–52; denied
temporal powers by Puri-
tans, 65–66, 68, 70–71, 79;
participate in English government, 66–67, 119; sup-
port of, 74–76, 110–112; influence in Massachusetts
government, 76–79; educa-
tion of, 112
Mohammedans, 95, 109
Moses, 94, 102, 128

New Testament, 90–93
Niantics, 122
Nineveh, 104
Nova Scotia, 121

Oaths, 31–32, 149
Office-holding: in Massachusetts, 70–71, 76, 117;
Williams' view of, 116–118,
129

Old Testament, 90–93
Ovid, 135

Pacifism, of Williams, 92, 93–
94, 96, 98, 100–101, 121–125
Papacy, see Roman Catholic
Church
Parliament, 49–50, 81, 94, 96–
97, 100–101, 111, 140
Paul, 21, 110, 112
Peace, 120–126
Pembroke Hall, Cambridge, 6
Pequot War, 122–123
Perkins, William, 47, 130–131
Persecution, 8, 100–101, 105–
106, 113
Peru, 134
Peter, 110, 112
Pilgrims, 22, 24, 26, 38, 81
Plymouth, Mass., 22, 24, 26,
38, 43, 81
Policy, 116
Pope, see Roman Catholic
Church
Prayer, 23, 27, 31, 32, 43, 44
Preaching: and redemption,
12, 41–42; and Separatism,
21–23, 41, 49; as part of wor-
ship, 30–31, 33; apostolic
and pastoral, 41–45; of
prophets in sackcloth, 50–51
Presbyterians, 56, 100, 154,
155
Profession of faith, 20, 34, 37
Prophesying, 21, 41, 50–51
Prophets in sackcloth, 50–52
Prosperity, 82, 107–114
Providence, R. I., 39, 53, 133
Public welfare, 127–128, 134–
135, 136–137